W9-BZL-284

SELLING IT

W. W. NORTON & COMPANY

NEW YORK · LONDON

The Incredible Shrinking Package and
Other Marvels of Modern Marketing

SELLING IT

BY LESLIE WARE
and the editors of
Consumer Reports

For information about permission to reproduce selections from this book, write to Permissions,
W. W. Norton & Company, Inc., 500 Fifth Avenue, New York, NY 10110

The text of this book is composed in Adobe Garamond with the display set in Trade Gothic
Composition by Carole Desnoes and Judith Abbate
Manufacturing by Phoenix Color Corp.
Book design by Judith Stagnitto Abbate/Abbate Design
Production manager: Amanda Morrison

Library of Congress Cataloging-in-Publication Data

Selling it : the incredible shrinking package and other marvels of modern marketing / by Leslie Ware
and the editors of Consumer reports.
p. cm.
ISBN 0-393-32172-X (pbk.)
1. Deceptive advertising. 2. Consumers. 3. Quality of products. I. Consumer reports. II. Title.

HF5827.8 .S45 2001
658.8—dc21   2001041004

W. W. Norton & Company, Inc., 500 Fifth Avenue, New York, N.Y. 10110
www.wwnorton.com

W. W. Norton & Company Ltd., Castle House, 75/76 Wells Street, London W1T 3QT

1 2 3 4 5 6 7 8 9 0

☆ ☆ ☆ ☆ ☆ ☆ ☆ ☆ ☆ ☆ ☆ ☆ ☆ ☆ ☆ ☆ ☆

★ ☆ ★ ☆ ★ ☆ ★ ☆ ★ ☆ ★ ☆ ★ ☆ ★ ☆ ★ ☆ ★ ☆ ★ ☆ ★ ☆

For my mother, Molly Blanchard Ware, whose sense of
fair play is equaled by her sense of humor.

With thanks to my husband, Phil Caputo, and to
Alex Markovich, Gordon Hard, and
Moye Thompson, former editors and writers of the
"Selling It" column, whose work appears
on some of these pages.

—Leslie Ware

☆ ☆ ☆ ☆ ☆ ☆ ☆ ☆ ☆ ☆ ☆ ☆ ☆ ☆ ☆ ☆ ☆ ☆ ☆

"The buyer needs a hundred eyes, the seller not one."

George Herbert, 1593–1633

INTRODUCTION

Sell 1. To exchange or deliver for money or its equivalent, as goods, services, or property; dispose of for a price. . . . 6. Slang. To cheat or dupe.

American Heritage Dictionary

Complete this sentence: As a buyer, you are (a) a puppet, (b) a grown-up, (c) a victim, (d) a fox, (e) a lemming.

As a test-taker, you are (f) a lucky devil: Each answer can be correct, and each has been suggested by a raft of social critics, advertising types, and economists. We at *Consumer Reports* prefer to see buyers as people who don't have time for such analyses, who are simply trying to tease out the difference between true and false: whether "10 free minutes" are actually going to cost you ten bucks; whether the "trial book" you've ordered will expand month by month into a library; whether you're truly a "guaranteed winner!"; whether those "slimming insoles" touted on TV do more than just cushion your tired feet.

There certainly isn't a shortage of come-ons to sort through. Estimates vary, but they suggest that the average American sees anywhere from 1,500 ads to 16,000 marketing messages (including logos) every day. Total U.S. advertising expenditures were expected to reach $250 billion in 2001. That's about $875 per American per year. And it equals the 1999 gross national product of Belgium.

Ads for seasick medicine adorn air-sickness bags, and beach sand, and rockets. Sometimes the placement of ads is positively undignified. Boats are named *EF Language* instead of *Queen Elizabeth,* and not long ago a financial web site considered asking its subscribers to affix little court-jester-hat stickers onto the heads of the presidents pictured on currency.

The power of advertising is indisputable. Consider the prune. Through advertising, two organizations—the California Prune Advisory Board and the Institute for Motivational Research—transformed a dark, squishy, wrinkled object stuck with an unfortunate image into something delightful and sweet, almost a candy. Not interested in prunes? How about cigarettes? Before 1954, Marlboros had a red-paper "beauty tip" to hide lipstick, came in a white pack that promised they were "Mild as May," and sold mostly to women. Then that cowboy loped into view and changed everything.

Still, advertising is not omnipotent. No less an authority than the Catholic Church has provided advertisers with special protection. In 1956, Pope Pius XII named Bernardino of Siena (1380–1444) the patron saint of advertising. Bernardino reportedly used simple language and effective symbols to convert many members of his audience. His silver tongue and the tablet he often carried, inscribed IHS (a graphic symbol for Jesus), won him the advertising gig. (We had to smile when, in the course of our saintly research, an Internet search engine invited us to "Comparison shop for Saint Bernardino.")

We may think we have it worse than our ancestors: that we're bombarded with more ads and need extra street smarts to decipher the new millennium's sales pitch. Not necessarily.

Ads were popping up everywhere as long ago as 1843, when English essayist Thomas Carlyle found fault with a precursor to the weinermobile. "The Hatter in the Strand of London, instead of making better felt-hats than another, mounts a huge lath-and-plaster Hat, seven-feet high, upon wheels; sends a man to drive it through the streets," he wrote. "He has not attempted to make better hats, as he was appointed by the Universe to do, and as with this ingenuity of his he could very probably have done; but his whole industry is turned to persuade us that he has made such!" What's more, our forebears were advertising anything and everything. In England centuries ago, Bartholomew's Fair promoted "a male child born with a bear on his back alive." (One can only surmise that the copywriter's descendant was P. T. Barnum, who touted the "Fiji Mermaid"—the head of a monkey sewn to the body of a fish.)

In addition to being ubiquitous, old ads could be at least as problematic as some are today. Modern medical "miracles" may be worthless, but centuries ago, sellers of snake oil used to boast that it was, really, snake oil—or, as one impotence cure advertised, "replete with the full and whole Virtues of [vipers]." In a case from 1906, nine infants died after being treated with Kopp's Baby's Friend, which was advertised innocuously enough as the "King of Baby Soothers" but contained an opiate, morphine sulfate. Koremlu, a depilatory cream sold in the early 1930s, had as its active ingredient thallium acetate, a rat poison. And don't forget the Radiendocrinator, a brainchild of one William J. A. Bailey. Recommended for everything from poor memory to pimples, it was advertised as a source of gamma rays that could "ionize the endocrine glands." More than seventy years ago, it sold for $1,000 (about $10,300 in today's dollars). And people bought it.

That's not to say all is now copacetic in the world of marketing. In 1998, the U.S. Food and Drug Administration reported, a woman testified that her husband, who had Alzheimer's disease, was cured with the wonders of Pure Emu Oil, touted as beneficial in the treatment of "arthritis . . . ulcers . . . cancer, heart trouble, diabetes and more." Once again, he was able to mow the grass, clean out the garage, weed the flower beds, and take his morning walk. (The FDA relieved emus everywhere by declaring the concoction an unapproved drug that should be barred from the U.S. market.)

Other marketing is milder. A sandwich shop might claim, "Freshest ingredients you can buy." A perfectly healthy man might appear on TV as an announcer intones, "This is the face of tuberculosis." An ad might show workers harvesting orange oranges even though oranges are often picked green.

Is this legal? Often, yes. The Federal Trade Commission, which regulates the advertising of most products and services, relies heavily on the context of a sales pitch and on how reasonable consumers would interpret it. According to the FTC, advertising must not be *deceptive*: Important performance details must not be presented so as to mislead consumers acting reasonably. Furthermore, advertising must not be *unfair*: It must not be likely to cause an injury that a consumer could not reasonably avoid and that is not outweighed by some overall benefit. If a company says it didn't mean to mislead? That's usually no excuse. Moreover, disclaimers in unreadable print don't make a commercial kosher. If there's a claim involved—say, "Most doctors recommend Hammerhead pain reliever"—advertisers must have objective evidence.

On the other hand—and the hands are pretty close together—the FTC gives mere "puffery" a pass. Puffery, an actual term in advertising law, is subjective, general exaggeration that almost no one would believe and which therefore doesn't require substantiation. Examples: "Frosted Flakes are great," "Things go better with Coke," "BMW is The Ultimate Driving Machine." As at least one ad pundit has pointed out, puffery is legal only if it doesn't work.

A company caught violating FTC standards can: be ordered to stop its wicked ways, told to substantiate future claims, or hit with civil penalties of up to millions of dollars. Occasionally, an individual is banned from an industry.

One rarely used recourse is the corrective ad. The FTC's first litigated corrective-ad case, in 1975, involved a forty-year-long ad campaign in which Warner-Lambert claimed that its mouthwash, Listerine, had medical benefits. The FTC ordered the company to spend about $10 million to tell consumers that the benefits weren't as promised. The second such case came in 1999, when the FTC ordered Novartis Corporation to spend $8 million to inform the public that Doan's Pills were no better than other analgesics in treating back pain. In between were a number of cases in which companies chose to settle FTC proceedings by voluntarily agreeing to run corrections on labels or in ads.

The FTC filed about 150 deception cases in 1999, but clearly those represent a grain of sand in a Sahara of iffy claims. The FTC doesn't have the staff to investigate every shady pitch. Moreover, its internal procedures can take years to complete and can be postponed further by appeals through federal courts. It took sixteen years of litigation, with eleven thousand pages of testimony and 150 exhibits, for the agency to excise the word Liver from Carter's Little Liver Pills. (The pills did nothing for the liver.)

The FTC isn't the only ad watchdog. Other federal agencies regulate ads for prescription drugs, financial institutions, airlines, communications companies, and food labels. Nongovernmental entities like the Better Business Bureau, and advertising groups themselves, have their own standards and sanctions. Absent any other recourse, one company can simply sue another if it feels its competitor's ads are misleading.

Problems with local ads are sometimes brushed off. "The observer who judges advertising to be perniciously manipulative is complaining about national advertising campaigns," wrote Daniel Pope, author of *The Making of Modern Advertising,* "not the flyers of local grocers." However, it's often local or regional flyers, signs, labels, or promotions that feed the "Selling It" column of *Consumer Reports.* They may not be perniciously manipulative, but little pitches that crop up everywhere are annoying in their own right—and are nimble enough to slip easily past the public's defense mechanisms. Furthermore, according to *American Advertising,* self-regulation has been least consistent locally. "If advertising is serious about healing its self-inflicted wounds," the publication pointed out, "it needs to address the problem at the local level." Usually, state attorneys general and local consumer-affairs offices are left to do the addressing.

For a summary of who governs what when it comes to selling—and where to go for help if you're sold a bill of goods—see "Who Ya Gonna Call?" on page 198.

Advertising has had its fans and foes from the start. While searching for an honest man, the Greek philosopher Diogenes apparently didn't even bother shining his lamp in one particular area. "The market," he noted, "is a place set apart where men may deceive each other." One scholar noted that advertising early in America's history was "considered an embarrassment . . . the unruly servant kept backstairs and never allowed into the front parlor." (It must be noted, though, that throughout American history, even respectable people didn't care. Paul Revere touted false teeth; Ben Franklin advertised his stove and a product named for his mother-in-law: Widow Read's Ointment for the Itch.)

Public opinion of advertising seems to have hit a high-water mark in 1959, when a survey by the Gallup Organization found that 75 percent of respondents generally liked advertising. By the 1970s, though, Americans' opinion was increasingly negative. A Harris survey in the mid-seventies found that nearly half of the public thought that most or all of TV advertising was seriously misleading; more than one-quarter had similar views about ads in other media.

Later surveys tended to be smaller and less representative, but they continued to indicate that although people may find advertising entertaining, they don't think highly of it. A 1999 poll showed that 74 percent of respondents "strongly" or "somewhat" believed that "most advertisements deliberately stretch the truth about the products they advertise." A national Gallup Poll of adults conducted in 2000 asked how respondents would rate the honesty and ethical standards of people in various fields. Advertising practitioners received marks of very high or high from only 10 percent of respondents.

What do advertisers think of consumers? In a 1955 issue of *Fortune,* William H. Whyte, Jr., quoted a veteran salesman's advice to him as he struggled to learn merchandising techniques at Vick Chemical Company: "Fella, you will never sell anybody anything until you learn one simple thing. The man on the other side of the counter is the *enemy.*" And the enemy hasn't always been respected. Adman Charles Austin Bates said, in the 1890s, "Advertisers should never forget that they are addressing stupid people." (Consumers got their revenge: Bates went broke investing in a patent medicine, Laxacola, that he couldn't sell.)

A succinct but illuminating example of what some marketers think of some buyers came from an Indiana reader of *Consumer Reports.* He sent us the customer copy of a service order he received from a national department store when he needed a part for his washing machine. The form had spaces in which the store's service representative had typed the customer's name, the service requested, and so on. What had the rep typed in the space labeled "Special Instructions"? *Customer Bites Big Time.*

The "Selling It" column began documenting such shenanigans in June 1977, with a note that "the excesses of the marketplace can be at once funny and cautionary." The first column took Whirlpool to task for a TV ad that used over-the-top patriotism and a soaring eagle to hawk appliances; bemoaned the arrest of a man who had accepted a supermarket's invitation to "check and compare" its prices with its competitors'; and made gentle fun of a tiny TV set, a funeral home offering drive-in wakes, and a 240-pound household robot.

Since then we've covered the gamut of selling strategies—some vicious, some questionable, some just humorous. We find most of the fodder for the column through *Consumer Reports* readers, a very dedicated lot and vigilant pack rats. Every month, readers send up to three hundred suggestions. We've received deodorant sticks, panty hose, a teaspoonful of dried soup secured under tape, even partially eaten pies. One submission, sent years ago, remains in the "Selling It" hall of fame: a severed steering wheel, complete with the lock-on bar that was supposed to keep the car from being stolen.

The editor is subjected to her share of gotchas, most in the line of duty. In covering the Scams Hotline, which purported to provide "essential information" about rip-offs, she paid $20 to find out that if a deal sounds too good to be true, it probably is, and that not all scams involve thousands of dollars. Duly noted.

Consumer Reports was even drawn into one of Hollywood's product-placement gambits. Castle Rock Entertainment, maker of the movie *Honeymoon in Vegas,* wrote a mention of the magazine into a scene, then informed us that companies usually pay $5,000 to $10,000 for that privilege. We didn't—and they kept us in.

Occasionally, a much-wanted item slips from our clutches. Several years ago, the "Selling It" editor provided information about her cat—his name, hair length, and breed—along with a check for $10, to one Urana Grey, "the true 21st Century Numerologist for Cats!" She was hoping to find out, as promised, "how your cat's Personality Vibration Number affects its behavior" and "what your Kitty-Kat is saying to you." Alas, the editor's check was returned, with a letter saying Ms. Grey was traveling and would be able to turn her attention to the cat only upon her return. Apparently, Ms. Grey is still traveling.

In future columns, we may find less to critique about telemarketers, who have been restrained somewhat by the Telemarketing and Consumer Fraud and Abuse Prevention Act. Signed by President Clinton in 1994, it strengthened the FTC's authority to prevent fraudulent or harassing telemarketing practices.

On the other hand, the Internet has opened up a new world for scam artists, and more and more people are getting caught in the web. Data from Consumer Sentinel, the FTC's database for consumer fraud, show a rapid rise in complaints related to on-line fraud and deception. In 1997, the database received fewer than 1,000 such complaints. In 2000, it received more than 25,000, roughly 26 percent of all the fraud complaints logged in.

In addition to alerting consumers about classic schemes that have migrated to the Internet—especially phony business opportunities, chain letters, health scams, free goods for a fee, cable descrambler kits, guaranteed loans or credit, credit-repair scams, and vacation prize promos—the FTC warns about "disguised advertising." That's a form of fraud in which comments about products or services posted on bulletin boards and in chat forums are sales pitches rather than objective information.

On a brighter note, the future is likely to bring an increase in mass customization—the widespread manufacture of products tailored to individuals. Ideally, that would shift power from a company to a person. Of course, advertisers would still advertise the basic products to be customized. And what of the nature of those products? In the Global Think Custom Conference of 2000, one session featured not a brave new world of useful products tailored to their owners' needs, but something a tad less lofty: MyDesign Barbie.

W atching pitches whiz by can be entertaining. So can buying, but not if you get burned. The collected wisdom about buying smart boils down to two points: Use common sense, and check the fine print. Nevertheless, there's a third point that's worth exploring: You can get scammed only if you agree to buy.

It's been said that advertising washes over us in places that aren't susceptible to rational thinking. People buy $1,000 watches when $40 models can keep time just as well; sports cars when sedans would be more sensible; horses because of a childhood memory. No less an advertising critic than Vance Packard, author of *The Hidden Persuaders,* acknowledged the appeal of such behavior. "When irrational acts are committed knowingly," he wrote, "they become a sort of delicious luxury." It's when someone is about to buy blindly—"under the influence" of advertising, as it were—that a reminder is in order. Just as you have the power to buy on a whim, you have the power not to buy. Refusal can take plenty of willpower in a culture that encourages consumption to excess—one whose economy is stoked when products are tossed and replaced. But after all, saying no is the ultimate hold you have over advertisers. They dangle the lure, but you don't have to bite.

Finally, a note about this book. It is not a philosophical treatise. We will not be examining advertising's persuasive powers "using the perspectives of utilitarianism, Kantian deontology, and virtue ethics," as one academic was recently said to have done. We won't be analyzing, as a marketing journal has, the literary device of metonymy in a misleading Listerine ad. Nor will we be demonizing every company and practice cited in these pages. While some pitches are truly nasty, others are simply amusing, and we've included both types. It's important to note that all the "Selling It" items are from past issues of *Consumer Reports* and are printed virtually as they appeared, along with their date of publication. The items refer to practices that existed at the time of original publication and shouldn't be understood as referring to the current practices of any of the companies named. Most of these ads—even some companies—no longer exist.

However, you needn't worry about a shortage of rip-offs, gaffes, malfeasance, malapropisms, misprints—and merriment. They're still out there. After all, when an e-commerce peddler of allergy-relief products invents a National Dust Mite Awareness Week, as one did in 2000, can a dryer company's Worldwide Lint Day be far behind?

CHAPTER 1

THIS MASQUERADE

"In the business arena, the challenge is to get your mailing past the mail room . . . then past 'White-fang,' the gate keeper in the outer office."
                                        Who's Mailing What, April 1998

In the household arena, *you* are White-fang, and like drugmakers who sugarcoat bitter pills, advertisers try to make their offers tasty enough that you'll swallow. One of the ruses we've often lampooned is the faux personal touch. Personalization, according to the trade publication *Inside Direct Mail,* is one of three techniques that have been proved to work repeatedly. (We'll get to the other two shortly.)

We've christened one persistent practitioner of personalization the Post-it bandit because he, she, it, or they often write billets-doux on a yellow sticky note. Our first glimpse of the bandit was in 1978, when several *Consumer Reports* readers received an ad that looked as if it had been torn from a business journal. The ad was for a book called *Common Sense Economics,* and on it was a seemingly handwritten note: "Really worth reading! R." Although the book was real, the business journal was not, and none of the readers had a clue who "R" was. Over the years, "R" occasionally morphed into "J," began using sticky notes to offer other publications, or addressed the recipient directly: "John, Try this. It work!" (an unfortunate grammatical lapse, considering this pitch was for a 566-page book on public speaking).

An especially galling attempt to be personal while inserting a foot in the door came in the form of a scrawled postcard sent in 1978. "Been trying to reach you," it said. "It's important to us that we talk to you. Please call me collect if necessary as soon as possible [a long-distance phone number followed]. Ask for me. Thank you, Marie Cole." On calling Ms. Cole, the recipient heard a pitch for magazine subscriptions.

Envelopes often exhibit the second of those three proven techniques—wearing the disguise of an official document. They lure with legalese and design elements that appear to have been stamped on. A "Rate Overpayment Notification" from the "Official Disbursement Division" offered a loan. A missive labeled "Internal Revenue Service Information" and "extremely urgent delivery, 48 hour reply requested" was from an outfit called the National Taxpayers Union, and the information inside was *about* the IRS.

Eagles are a favorite official-looking symbol. A folded card picturing a bald eagle and featuring the phrases "hand deliver only," "extremely urgent," and "dated material enclosed," along with an account number and a package number, related to cable TV service. (The man who received it reported that the mail carrier did indeed hand-deliver it, along with the rest of his mail.)

In 1990, after government look-alike mailings got out of hand, Congress declared that solicitations using any symbol or name that could reasonably be construed as implying a connection with the federal government could not be mailed unless they bore a disclaimer. The statute decreased the volume of official fakes; however, the envelope eagle is by no means an endangered species.

Sometimes envelopes wear nonofficial disguises that prove equally alluring. One we saw was marked "Photos of familiar faces inside," and you might have thought it was a cute photo mailer bought by relatives. No, these photos were of a smiling generic family—mom, dad, boy, and spotted dog—with a pitch for insurance. If a tug at the heartstrings doesn't work, perhaps something to make you worry? An envelope from Bolero Medical Associates marked "X-ray enclosed" and "Confidential Patient Information" did enclose what looked very much like an X-ray. It showed a human skull, and it touted a clear bowling ball with a skull facsimile inside.

To quote *Inside Direct Mail*: "Be careful with the teaser copy on your outer envelope. You may not draw the attention of any state attorneys general or the FTC, but you could achieve an equally negative outcome: Turning off potential prospects who bad-mouth your company to everyone they know." Well, yes.

The contents of those envelopes can carry on the ruse. One of the nastiest fakes is the masquerade bill. If a mailing looks like a bill but is actually a pitch for business, U.S. Postal Service regulations require it to identify itself as a solicitation. The disclosure is supposed to be in conspicuous and legible type, but guess what? It almost never is. An outfit called Sony Industries sent a Michigan corporation a mock invoice for sixty fluorescent tubes, for $995. The words "this is a solicitation" were about the size of the type on this page and were buried in two lines of information at the bottom of an eight-by-ten-inch sheet. A school in California received a mock invoice for Poly Liners, one hundred units, for $988.60. Anyone missing the minuscule disclaimer would apparently have bought 100 plastic bags for $9.88 each.

If you've escaped the Scylla of the fake bill, don't relax yet. There's still the Charybdis of the phony check—the third of the three proven techniques, says *Inside Direct Mail*: "Fake checks, in particular, seem to work because they get the prospect to open the mailing in the belief that easy money is waiting inside. Of course, what appears to be a check is really just the top part of a letter that explains how the prospect could qualify for a loan in that amount." Or, even more annoying, it's a real check that hooks you once endorsed. In one instance, by cashing one $3.50 check, businesses could have unwittingly agreed to $150 worth of Internet advertising. Generally, only fine print provides a warning.

Again, *Inside Direct Mail*: "Despite their persuasive powers to motivate prospects to open the envelope, fake checks can backfire on you. Prospects may feel cheated when they realize the check is not real." Hmm—the marketers may be on to something here.

Products themselves wear other disguises—the Stars and Stripes, for instance. Companies usually don't have to disclose whether or how much of their product is made in the United States, but for those that choose to claim "Made in USA," the Federal Trade Commission says that all or virtually all of the product must indeed have been made in the United States. Whether a phrase or symbol implies a claim of origin depends upon the context. Ordinarily the FTC won't count the use of an American brand name or trademark alone as a U.S.-origin claim. (After all, the agency points out, just because a few misguided souls may think Danish pastry is made in Denmark doesn't mean you can't call pastry "Danish.") On the other hand, if a product uses symbols inappropriately, the agency may crack down. In one case involving a maker of CD-ROM drives, the FTC alleged that although the packaging included a red, white, and blue flag, an eagle, and the Statue of Liberty, most of the parts were imported. (The company admitted no violation of the law, but if it makes such implied claims again, it can be fined.)

Other companies lay it on nearly as thick. In 1992, we razzed the American Eagle Collector's Commemorative Pocket Knife, which extolled "this majestic bird . . . the foremost symbol of freedom in the world!" The knife, "exclusively from the American International Mint," was made in Taiwan. Two years later, a reader sent us a plastic bag labeled with the large words "Made in Oregon"—the actual name of a company whose products were all "made, caught, or grown in Oregon." The bag itself? Made in that farthest outpost of Oregon—China.

To appear patriotic, car dealers have been known to do everything short of honking out the national anthem. "Buying American is a patriotic decision!" one dealer said in a 1991 newspaper ad. "Buying a foreign car is strictly a political decision." The ad then claimed the automobile as a "purely American" achievement.

Auto historians, however, have another opinion. They generally credit two German engineers, Gottlieb Daimler and Karl Benz, with building the first practical cars more than a century ago. Moreover, among the models listed in this particular ad was the Ford Festiva. It was made in Korea. In this era of automotive Esperanto—when Volvo, for instance, is based in Göteborg, Sweden, is owned by Ford, and has its S40 made in Holland using a platform shared with the Mitsubishi Carisma—country of origin might be less important than quality and price.

When a foreign name has a certain cachet, it can be invoked to cover a product's less-resonant origins. We noted that a can of Progresso tomatoes labeled "Progresso Tipo Italiano, Progresso makes it Italian! Pomodori pelati con basilico" was indeed *importati,* but from Chile, not Italy. We saw "Traditional Swedish bread" made in Germany, and Papa Nino's pasta, labeled "Italian style" and bearing the colors of the Italian flag, but a "Product of Turkey." And what is one to make of La chemise cacharel, whose hang tag reads, "What makes it a truly French Shirt? Made in Hong Kong."

These kinds of masquerades may be the most visible in daily life, but they're a mere Batman mask compared with the full-body gorilla suit of other ruses. Big companies spin off what a columnist for *Advertising Age* has called "fake little companies," a practice that began when E&J Gallo Winery had two good old boys hawk wine coolers under the fictitious Bartles & Jaymes banner.

Advertorials—magazine advertising sections with lots of text—can be another disguise. Then there's the magalog or maybe catazine, a magazine that looks like a catalog. In another variant, public-relations firms submit articles and TV spots on consumer-helpful subjects but with a twist: They've inserted a product plug. In a Wyoming newspaper, for instance, *Consumer Reports* found a PR agency's article about wintertime care for lips "on the mistletoe circuit." It recommended using a lip ointment "such as Blistex."

Informercials are an easy target, and they're being joined by even odder amalgamations, including the dramatisement. For example, an ad campaign for Ford trucks spawned a series of adventure-sportsTV shows produced by Ford and touting Ford vehicles during the real commercials that interrupted each hour-long pseudocommercial. Then there's the moviemercial, which is what results when well-known directors feature BMWs in short films that are shown on the car company's web site.

In an insidious masquerade, ads wrap themselves in education. Perhaps the best-known example is Channel One, the advertising-supported news program watched by about eight million children in about twelve thousand schools. The schools get a satellite dish, TV sets, and a closed-circuit TV system. The kids get ten minutes of news per day and two minutes of commercials. Over a school year, the ads kill about six hours of class time.

Companies may supply schools with drinks or sportswear under exclusive contracts; reward them for having students collect product labels; sponsor instructional materials; even pay to place company logos on school rooftops. Where this interaction can lead became evident in 1998, when Greenbrier High in Evans, Georgia, declared a Coke in Education Day to vie for a prize the Coca-Cola Company offered. The school invited a Coke executive to discuss his job, had chemistry students measure Coke's sugar content, had home-ec students follow a Coke cake recipe, and asked all its students to wear Coke T-shirts and spell out C-O-K-E for a school photo. Amid all the red-and-white shirts, student Mike Cameron's blue-and-white Pepsi shirt stood out like a dandelion on a putting green.

The bad news is that Cameron was suspended. The good news is that there was such an uproar, his suspension was suspended. The further bad news is that this kind of thing isn't surprising anymore. It seems money can turn some people's heads so far they don't even notice a gorilla in their midst. > > >

Winning by intimidation

This envelope, from the "Community Protection (Nuclear) Department" is one of the more egregious examples of the "official government" masquerade.

The "Official Hazard Warning" inside the envelope features an American eagle and the legend "Buy U.S. savings bonds." The prose hints darkly that "failure to reply immediately . . . puts the Recipient . . . at HIGH RISK to health." What's it all about? It's pitch for a $23 radon-detector.

You'd never know that from the somewhat fractured governmentese: "As a responsible Citizen of the United States…it is encumbant [sic] upon you to consider the $20 laboratory Testing Fee as Health Hazard Protection." Evidently we're supposed to think that buying the device is a patriotic duty.

—July 1990

Gotcha

Home Centers, a chain of Ohio appliance-and-audio stores, sent this envelope to customers, one of whom was a subscriber. He opened it right away to find out which of his appliances was malfunctioning. The letter inside showed that the recall was just a gimmick: The chain was "recalling" its old name and changing to a new one. We won't reward this little ploy by mentioning the new name. So there.

—March 1992

Intimations of mortality

With the eagle, the Old American name, and the reference to Social Security benefits, you might be forgiven for thinking this heading signals an important update from the government. Instead, it's a pitch for a whole-life insurance policy to help cover funeral costs. Tip-offs: a small footnote, "We are not affiliated with any government agency," and an ominous return address, Final Expense Information Center.

—August 1995

Dollars and census

The "census" mailing just happened to arrive at census time. It was really an ad for mail-order pants from Haband, in Paterson, New Jersey.

As for the envelope with the federal eagle and the "savings bonds" inscription, it was an invitation to endure a sales pitch for resort time-sharing at Westwood Villas in Pennsylvania. A subtle touch: At first glance, the large "25" in the upper right corner looks like the amount of postage paid, but it's really the number of the meter permit. Tiny vertical print that says "BLK. RT." is the giveaway.

—May 1990

A pitch by any other name

"Junk" mail is forever dressing up to fool the recipient into overestimating its worth. Lately, we've seen some especially inventive disguises. Here, the sheep's clothing, and the wolf.

1. Inside: "Park your savings" in certificates of deposit from California-based World Savings.

2. Inside: Enjoy "the Infiniti total ownership experience" provided by Koeppel Infiniti of Queens, New York. (Koeppel enclosed an X-ray-like image of the car but failed to reveal the link between X-rays and ownership experience.)

3. Inside: "Add ease, efficiency, and economy to hotel selection" with "Hotel and Travel Index."

4. Inside: Send "as much as you can afford" to stop President Clinton's health-care plan.

—November 1994

Mystery mail

"Eugene, Try it. It's only ½ price! R." read the handwritten note a California reader (called Gene by everybody but R) recently found in his mailbox. Apparently, R has a lot of pals. He or she has sent other readers in California, Delaware, and New York the same personal appeal. Each tip arrived on a yellow sticky note in a plain white envelope, postmarked Santa Ana, California. And each was attached to what appeared to be a newspaper clipping—a rave review of Gero Vita GH3 Famous Romanian Anti-Aging Formula, packed with names and photos of endorsing physicians from Duke University, UCLA Medical School, and other reputable institutions.

Conveniently located on the flip side of the "article" were testimonials and an ad for Gero Vita GH3, complete with a toll-free order number and a mailing address in Phoenix, Arizona. (Gero Vita GH3 is apparently an "improved" version of Gerovital H3, a drug whose active agent was best known as Novocain.)

Officials at Duke and UCLA told us they've never heard of the doctors cited in the clipping. But the Better Business Bureau of Phoenix has heard plenty about Gero Vita GH3 and its parent company, Vita Industries. Records show that the company has a history of failing to deliver products and promised refunds and has engaged in "questionable business practices," including deceptive advertising with bogus articles and yellow sticky notes.

As for that famous formula that R is so eager to sell, the Better Business Bureau says it's a harmless dietary supplement, available over-the-counter for one-tenth the price charged by Vita Industries.

—*February 1993*

I took the original Gerovital for the last ten years and am now taking your improved GH3. I am 66 years old... and have no gray hair, I do not wear glasses, I have no receding hair or balding. I can [...] whenever I choos[...] wrinkles or doubl[...] no brown age s[...] hands. My short[...] is as good as it [...]

Eugene,
TRY IT.
IT'S ONLY
½ PRICE!
R

That personal touch

More and more companies, it seems, are trying to give mass mailings a handmade look. Here's the work of the envelope doodler, from First Union National Bank, in Charlotte, North Carolina. Our favorite touch: the coffee stain.

—*June 1996*

An xxxintentional goof

Recently, one of our staffers received a missive from the Democratic National Committee that added an amusing twist to "handwritten" charades. With a nice touch of verisimilitude, the addressing machinery actually crossed out the first street number it "wrote." (The DNC told us the job was done by a Washington, D.C., company.)

And the official-looking "DPS AirBill"—is that an express-mailer? No, our contact at the DNC said, it just looks like one.

—December 1995

A pen pal reappears

Our old adversary the Post-it bandit is still at it, only he or she has changed names and careers. In February 1993, we reported several sightings of yellow sticky notes with customized, seemingly handwritten messages. These days, the notes are signed by "J" (J's writing varies from note to note) and stuck on a book review that touts either "American Speaker" or "Business Finance Advisor." Both books are sold by Georgetown Publishing House, in Washington, D.C.

The review looks as if it's been torn out of a magazine (the left edge is even ragged), but the publication's name never appears, and the publication date varies. Apparently this magazine runs the same review in every issue. The cost: $297 for one book plus several updates.

The Better Business Bureau says Georgetown's marketing tactics are misleading and has asked the company to stop using notes and tearsheets. Georgetown disagrees and has refused the bureau's request. For now, it's still up to the consumer to beware of J's friendly little jottings.

—November 1995

Pay at your peril

This General Lighting Company "bill," for $960, got through two levels of screening at a Massachusetts company before someone in the accounting department noticed a note at the bottom: "This is not a bill," it says. "This is a solicitation."

—February 1996

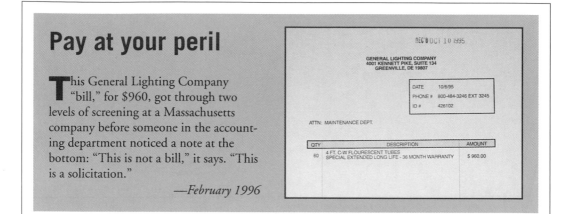

Pay at your peril, part 2

When Bon Secours-St. Mary's Health Corporation of Richmond, Virginia, began receiving what looked like bills for classified ads it had placed, its bookkeeping department paid automatically—to the tune of more than $1,500. The statements, which were similar but came from two different organizations, summarized each ad— "Registered nurses—emergency full time evening," for instance. At the bottom of the page, the recipient was told to "Make check payable to" either Professional Employer or Employment Classifieds, both based in California.

The only problem was that St. Mary's hadn't placed the ads: The bills weren't bills; they were solicitations. That's explained on the statement above in large but virtually unreadable yellow-on-green type. With persistence,

St. Mary's got its money back, but the mailings haven't stopped—within about a month, St. Mary's received fifteen more. "I can't tell you," a spokesperson said, "how incensed I get every time I see one come through."

When we called Professional Employer, an employee said that if we accepted a solicitation, our ad would be put in a publication that is "like a newspaper" and "goes all over the country."

—January 1994

Wave the flag and up the circulation

The bill look-alike below didn't fool a Massachusetts reader, but he was struck by the sentence on its reverse side (underlining ours). Worse still, the reader adds, the solicitation is for a magazine he already receives—at a lower rate.

—June 1997

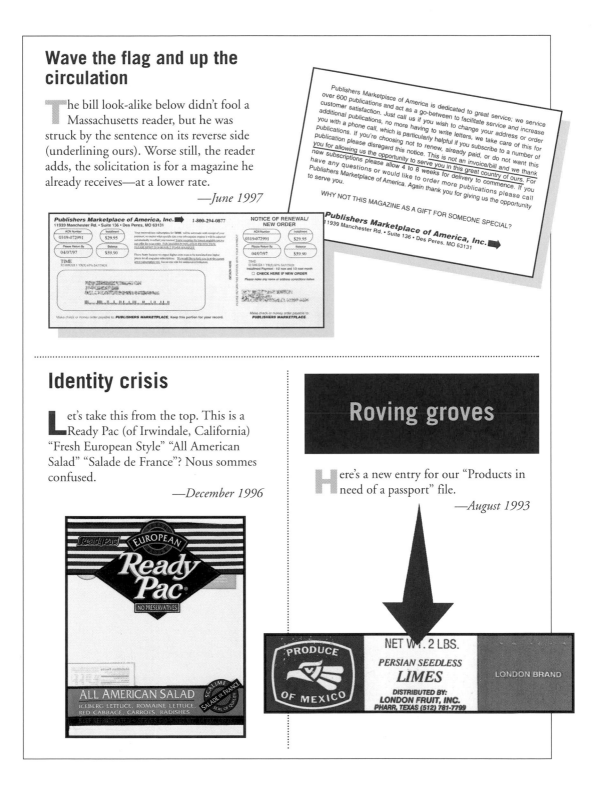

Publishers Marketplace of America is dedicated to great service; we service over 600 publications and act as a go-between to facilitate service and increase customer satisfaction. Just call us if you wish to change your address or order additional publications, no more having to write letters, we take care of this for you with a phone call, which is particularly helpful if you subscribe to a number of publications. If you're choosing not to renew, already paid, or do not want this publication please disregard this notice. This is not an invoice/bill and we thank you for allowing us the opportunity to serve you in this great country of ours. For new subscriptions please allow 4 to 8 weeks for delivery to commence. If you have any questions or would like to order more publications please call Publishers Marketplace of America. Again thank you for giving us the opportunity to serve you.

WHY NOT THIS MAGAZINE AS A GIFT FOR SOMEONE SPECIAL?

Publishers Marketplace of America, Inc. ▶
11939 Manchester Rd. • Suite 136 • Des Peres. MO 63131

Identity crisis

Let's take this from the top. This is a Ready Pac (of Irwindale, California) "Fresh European Style" "All American Salad" "Salade de France"? Nous sommes confused.

—December 1996

Roving groves

Here's a new entry for our "Products in need of a passport" file.

—August 1993

The toast of many towns

European-style New York Texas Garlic Toast made in Columbus, Ohio? Ooh la, la. Fuhgeddaboutit. Ya-HOO. Buonissimo.
    And gosh.

—November 1997

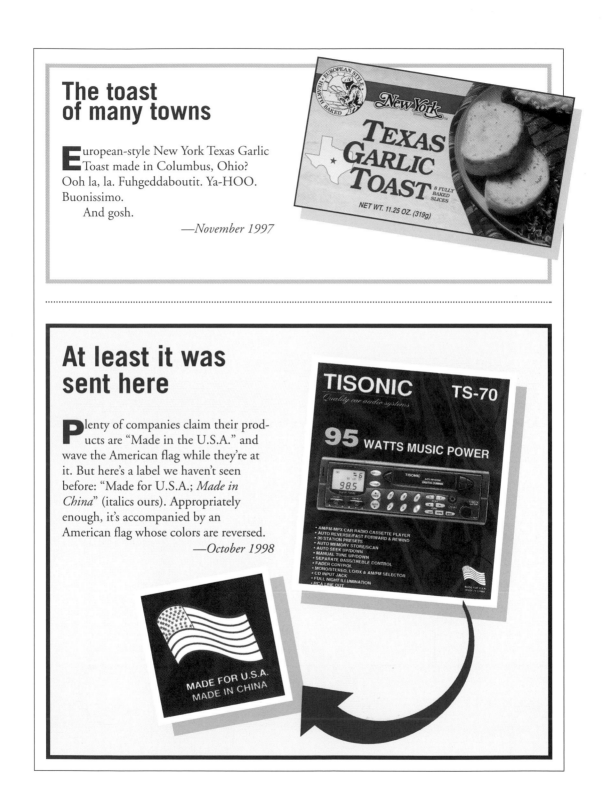

At least it was sent here

Plenty of companies claim their products are "Made in the U.S.A." and wave the American flag while they're at it. But here's a label we haven't seen before: "Made for U.S.A.; *Made in China*" (italics ours). Appropriately enough, it's accompanied by an American flag whose colors are reversed.

—October 1998

Patriot games

The American Patriot Whistle, all decked out in red, white, and blue, is sold by the American Whistle Corporation and "Crafted with Pride in the USA." A squint at the whistle itself reveals that it's actually crafted an ocean away from the fifty states. A call to the company confirmed that the whistle is made in Taiwan—it's just packaged in the U.S.

—March 1998

Starred and striped

This "USA Flag Jacket," from a catalog called The Sportsman's Guide, has "USA lettering, leather flag stripes down both sleeves and a complete leather USA flag on the back . . . which in turn is highlighted by richly embroidered stars." Anyone can see it's "As American as apple pie!" But anyone with good eyes can also look farther down in the description and see the word "Imported."

—July 1994

Close Thais to America?

Perhaps I. C. Isaacs, whose clothing came with this tag, means that those Americans are working in Thailand.

—July 1994

"Keeping Americans Working"

MADE IN THAILAND

Lead astray

The no-commercialization policy at *Consumer Reports* states that "neither the Ratings nor the reports may be used in advertising or for any other commercial purpose." But sometimes companies don't pay attention, to either the policy or the truth. A recent example (below) was especially egregious. It's represented to be our February 1993 Listings of lead-removing water-treatment devices, showing six Equinox products leading their respective categories. The catch: We didn't test any Equinox products.

Someone doctored the page, inserting the names of the Equinox devices and going so far as to add a category we didn't test—whole house systems—in which Equinox stood alone. The real page is opposite. One tip-off: Apparently, the new typesetter couldn't get the hang of our little better-to-worse circles, called "blobs" by staffers. As a result, the word "easy" appears in the next-to-last column.

Equinox denies any responsibility and blames the doctoring on rogue distributors over which it has no control.

—*August 1994*

Brand and model	Price	Operating cost	Lead removed	Life, mfr.	Minutes per gallon	Ease of installation
WHOLE HOUSE SYSTEMS						
EQ-300 Equinox Whole House	$1,259	$8	99%	300,000 gal.	7 sec.	easy	J
REVERSE-OSMOSIS DEVICES						
...n Aqualeer H-63 system	$750	50	98	3-5 yr.	180	●	A,F,J
...Kenmore 3490	399	45	99	3 yr.	120	●	A,E,C
...LERS						
...lenmore Distiller 3450	100	237	99	--	420	○	G,R
...SINK FILTERS						
EQ-15 Equinox Under Counter	294	8	99	15,000/8 yrs. (at 5 gal. per day)	1	easy	J,B
EQ-2 Equinox In-Line	60	0	99	2,000 gal.	2	easy	
Everpure QC4-VOC	312	226	92	500 gal./1 yr.	2.8	◕	J
Multipure MPC500B	330	76	92	500 gal./1 yr.	1.6	◔	J
Omni Total Plus OT-5	160	66	86	1 yr.	1.1	◕	--
Selecto Lead-Out 20	85	12	88①	5,000 gal.	0.3	○	H,K
Teledyne Water Pik Instapure 100	189	44	92	1,200 gal./1 yr.	1.6	○	B
COUNTERTOP FILTERS						
EQ-10 Equinox Countertop	200	0	99	10,000 gal./5 yrs (at 5 gal. per day)	1.2	easy	J
Ametek Water Filter CT CMR-10	65	36	88	750 gal./1 yr.	2.3	◒	--
Amway Water Treatment System E-9225	227	110	90	750 gal./1 yr.	0.6	◒	I,J
Sterling Spring CTS	119*	25	81①	1 yr.	1.8	◒	P
■ The following two models became clogged very early in their expected life.						
Bionaire H2O BT-820	100*	②	99	700 gal./1 yr.	2.5	◒	D,L,C
Club Watermaster's K6795ASF	499	②	99	700 gal./1 yr.	2.8	◒	J,M
FAUCET FILTERS						
EQ-40 Equinox Shower Mate	125	0		40,000 gal.	20 sec.	easy	
Nordic Ware 78100	76	67	83	3 mo.	1.6		N
CARAFE FILTERS						
EQ-1 Equinox Traveler	50	0		1,000 gal	2	easy	
Brita Water Filter System 0B01/0B03	25	230	86	35 gal./1-2 mo.	20	○	C,J
NOT ACCEPTABLE						
■ During our tests, the following model removed only 50 percent of the lead.						
Glacier Pure Water Filter 62290	10	100	50	50 gal.	60	◒	C

attach to the existing faucet by flexible tubing. **Faucet-mounted filters** attach to and perch atop the existing faucet. **Carafe filters** sit on a counter or table; you simply pour water through them. Water-treatment devices are generally available at home centers and plumbing-supply stores. If you

filters, including any that remove contaminants other than lead, are changed at the manufacturer's recommended interval.

4 Lead-removal system. For most devices, this is a filter, but reverse-osmosis devices and distillers use mechanisms other than filtration to remove lead (see page

...fy a gallon of water. Figures for reverse-osmosis devices assume the storage tank has been depleted.

Ease of installation. Carafe filters and distillers operate pretty much right out of the box; other devices require plumbing tasks from simple to intricate.

1 Brand and model	2 Price	3 Operating cost	4 Lead-removal system		5 Minutes per gallon	6 Ease of installation	Comments
			Lead removed	Life, mfr.			
Reverse-osmosis devices							
Culligan Aquacleer H-83 System	$750	$50	98%	3-5 yr.	180	●	A,F,J
Sears Kenmore 3490	399	45	99	3 yr.	120	●	A,E,Q
Distillers							
Sears Kenmore Distiller 3450	100	237	99	—	420	◓	G,R
Undersink filters							
Everpure QC4-VOC	312	226	92	500 gal./1 yr.	2.8	◒	J
Multipure MPC500B	330	76	92	500 gal./1 yr.	1.6	◒	J
Omni Total Plus OT-5	160	66	86	1 yr.	1.1	◒	—
Selecto Lead-Out 20	85	12	88 [1]	5000 gal.	0.3	◒	H,K
Teledyne WaterPik Instapure 100	189	44	92	1200 gal./1 yr.	1.6	○	B
Countertop filters							
Ametek Water Filter CT CMR-10	65	36	88	750 gal./1 yr.	2.3	◔	—
Amway Water Treatment System E-9225	227	110	90	750 gal./1 yr.	0.6	◔	I,J
Sterling Spring CTS	119*	25	81 [1]	1 yr.	1.8	◔	P
■ The following two models became clogged very early in their expected life.							
Bionaire H2O BT-820	100*	[2]	99	700 gal./1 yr.	2.5	◔	D,L,O
Club Watermaster's K6795ASF	499	[2]	99	700 gal./1 yr.	2.8	◔	J,M
Faucet filters							
Nordic Ware 78100	76	67	83	3 mo.	1.8	◔	N
Carafe filters							
Brita Water Filter System OB01/OB03	25	230	86	35 gal./1-2 mo.	20	◓	C,J
Not Acceptable							
■ During our tests, the following model removed only 50 percent of the lead.							
Glacier Pure Water Filter 62290	10	100	50	50 gal.	60	◓	C

[1] Although they performed well overall, these models removed much less lead in a few test runs than they did in all other test runs.
[2] Not calculated. Because the filters clogged quickly with our test water, replacement costs would be very high.

Key to Comments
A–Stores purified water in 2.7-gal. tank.
B–Easiest to install of undersink models.
C–Stores purified water in 1-gal. carafe.
D–Mfr. specifies minimum line pressure of 65 psi., above what we consider typical minimum household pressure.
E–Wastes 15 gal. of water per day.
F–Wastes 30 gal. of water per day; automatic shut-off valve is optional.
G–Consumes electrical energy; operating cost based on average U.S. cost of 8¼ cents per kilowatt-hour.
H–Needs tubing, connections, spigot; not included.
I–Needs tubing, connections; not included.
J–Certified by National Sanitation Foundation.
K–Couldn't confirm manufacturer's claim for filter life. Our test went only 1000 gal.
L–Clogged at 100 gal.
M–Clogged at 150 gal.
N–Clogged at 200 gal.
O–Discontinued.
P–Discontinued. Replaced by **Sterling Spring CTD**, $100.
Q–Also sold as **Ecowater ERO-300.**
R–Also sold as **Ecowater Distiller 10001.**

82

CONSUMER REPORTS FEBRUARY 1993CONSUMER REPORTS FEBRUARY 1993

THIS MASQUERADE 15THIS MASQUERADE 15

An immortal author

Hastening through an airport bookstore recently, one of our readers grabbed what looked like the latest book by Alistair MacLean, author of such popular adventure novels as *The Guns of Navarone*. The paperback is a Fawcett Crest book from Ballantine Books, a division of Random House. What caught our reader's eye were the prominent words "Bestselling Author Alistair MacLean's Night Watch." What didn't catch his eye was the smaller type at the bottom: "Written by Alastair MacNeill." Alistair MacLean died in 1987. A postscript on the last page of *Night Watch* says that when MacLean died, "he left behind several outlines for novels." These were used by one Alastair MacNeill as the basis for "Alistair MacLean's *Night Watch*" and "Alistair MacLean's *Death Train*." Fawcett Books told us Alastair MacNeill is a real author.

Our reader found *Night Watch* disappointing. He prefers the real McCoy—er, MacLean.

—*July 1991*

The game's afoot

"As a long-time Lawrence Sanders fan, I was delighted to see this latest novel on sale this summer," a reader told us. "But by the time I was about 20 pages into the book, I was struck that something was odd about the writing style." A search of the back cover revealed the usual blurbs: "Passion, greed, murder, and wit—they are Sanders's stock in trade."

The back flap, however, noted that Sanders "*was* the author [emphasis ours] of more than twenty-two bestsellers." Armed with the knowledge that Sanders had died (last year, it turns out), you might then think that he completed the book before his death. Not so fast, Sherlock; get out the magnifying glass. On an inside page, in tiny type, is this note: "The publisher and the estate of Lawrence Sanders have chosen Vincent Lardo to create this novel based on Lawrence Sanders's beloved character Archy McNally and his fictional world."

—*December 1999*

Reality bites

From the front of the box, you might conclude that Flee-Away Pet Wipes make fleas flee from pets. Not necessarily. Had you brought a magnifying glass to the store, you would have noticed the strategically placed word "irritation," as well as a tiny-type phrase at the box's base: "Does not kill fleas or ticks."

—*January 1995*

★ ☆ ★ ☆ ★ ☆ ★ ☆ ★ ☆ ★ ☆ ★ ☆ ★ ☆ ★ ☆ ★ ☆ ★ ☆ ★ ☆ ★ ☆

CHAPTER 2

FIRE THE COPYWRITER!

"Advertisements are now so numerous that they are very negligently perused, and it is therefore become necessary to gain attention by magnificence of promises, and by eloquence sometimes sublime and sometimes pathetic."

Dr. Samuel Johnson, *The Idler*

Ever since 1477, when the first ad was printed in English (it touted a book about the conduct of religious services and sold at a price "good chepe"), sellers have been searching for the perfect pitch. Although advertisers spent a reported $76 million in 2000 to track brand recognition after ad campaigns and to pretest TV ad copy—and advertisers can assess buyers' brain waves and skin reaction in more subtle ways than ever—no one can say for sure what techniques actually work.

P. T. Barnum prospered by bold, loud exaggeration. Other marketers have been quieter, more believable, even charming, although John E. Kennedy, writing in the 1890s, ventured awfully far into the rose garden in lauding Hudson's Bay department store in Winnipeg. "Aye, a veritable fairyland!" he wrote. "Looking down long avenues of dress fabrics and through dreamy, hazy vistas of cloudy laces and shimmering silks, which rival in coloring and variety the wealth of summer and autumn's rich array. . . ."

Early ads resembled comic strips or were serialized in stories that were a big hit with the public. The trade publication *Printer's Ink* reported that an ad campaign in 1902 made "Sunny Jim"—a formerly gloomy fellow supposedly transformed by Force breakfast cereal—as famous as Theodore Roosevelt, who happened to be president at the time.

Repetition worked for a while. In Frederick Wakeman's *The Hucksters,* published in 1946, the character Evan Llewelyn Evans notes, "Two things make good advertising. One, a good simple idea. Two, repetition. And by repetition, by God, I mean until the public is so irritated with it, they'll buy your brand because they bloody well can't forget it." Surely that was the case in 1949, when Pepsi's jingle "Pepsi Cola hits the spot. 12 full ounces, that's a lot!" was reportedly played 296,426 times on 469 radio stations.

When repetition palled, copywriters tried novelty. Or they returned to what was called reason-why advertising—a logical, unadorned argument for buying a particular product that could be reinforced with a slogan like "It floats." In the 1950s, the buzz acronym was U.S.P., for unique selling proposition. The coinage of adman Rosser Reeves, a U.S.P. was one strong claim that competitors couldn't make. Reeves mocked ads that came equipped with "a little deluge of adjectives" or those in which bears capered on food cans, products wore crowns, or cakes grew to monstrous dimensions. His idea of a good line: "Stops Halitosis!"

Be dignified, copywriters have been told over the years. No, be funny. Ignore the competition. Blast the competition. Imitate the competition. Don't use cute tricks. Do use cute tricks, whether they're 3-D glasses, party poppers, or microchips playing Christmas carols. Rely on market research. Don't. Sell the product hard. Stay low-key. ("To try to bludgeon your reader into a purchase reminds me of the story of the father of Frederick the Great," wrote Victor O. Schwab in *How to Write a Good Advertisement.* "He noticed that his subjects were dodging him in the streets. So he struck one of them with his whip and cried, 'Damn it, I want you to love me!' ")

In moving through these phases, copywriters have circled back to certain tried-and-true themes. Unfortunately, those tend to prey on the baser impulses to which humans are prone: lust, of course, but also fear, jealousy, and ambition.

Early on, scare ads often targeted women, who were supposed to be afraid they'd never get a man, possibly because of bad breath. A Listerine ad pictured a woman cradling a small dog. "What she *really* wanted," the copy read, "was Children." Copywriter Arthur Kudner famously invented a new name for *Tinea trichophyton,* a ringworm fungus, and wrote this headline for Absorbine Jr.: "His heart quickened at the soft fragrance of her cheeks, but her shoes hid a sorry case of athlete's foot." Another ad pictured an attractive young woman jumping a horse over a fence. Behind that image, however, was a dark shadow. It showed a woman twice as heavy, and her horse was balking at the fence. The moral: Better to smoke Lucky Strikes than to eat candy.

Once a woman had a man, her worries did not abate. "People whispered," blared an early ad for Wonder Bread, because a husband ate in town, not at home. "Tasteless 'bargain bread' was to blame." If a mom didn't feed her kids oatmeal, a Quaker ad hinted, they could be headed to the poorhouse or prison.

Men had their own worries. "Keep an eye on your wife!" cried an ad for Gillette razor blades. "Possibly she's not as happy as she seems." The trouble? "There is a chance she's distressed because you aren't as careful about shaving as you were in times past. . . ." Another ad pictured a brunette, her eyes averted, perched on a sofa beside an earnest-looking man. The headline: "And he wonders why she said 'NO!' " Turns out she couldn't stand his droopy socks.

Body odor was an equal-opportunity fear—or the more impressive nose pores and pimples (or, in ad-speak, "comedones"). A toilet soap warned every woman to take to heart the lesson provided by a dancer who had collapsed and died onstage from—drum roll here—clogged pores. Those scourges were joined by germy doorknobs, lapsed insurance policies, and a condition called toilet-tissue illness about which we'll write no more. Suffice to say copywriters were inventing reasons for consumers to lose sleep—and then, you can be sure, hyping a remedy for sleeplessness.

Speaking of comedones, a 1930s ad-spoof magazine called *Ballyhoo* published a list of euphemisms favored by copywriters, along with translations:

> *Lifetime* = until the new model comes out
> *Delicate membrane* = any part of the body
> *Lubricate the skin texture* = put on grease
> *Pore-deep cleansing* = washing the face
> *Harsh irritants* = all the ingredients of a competitor's product
> *Great scientist* = anyone who will sign an endorsement
> *Exclusive* = expensive

Nowadays, some ad copy has swung toward the literary and surreal. The self-effacing underclaim (picturing a Volkswagen Beetle with the label "Lemon") has evolved into no claim at all—which at least won't leave skeptics in its wake. As *ADWEEK* has pointed out, when an ad says "Think different" or asks "Got milk?" disbelief doesn't arise as one of your options.

One newer buzz term—"under the radar"—refers to an ad that supposedly penetrates consumers' defenses against the hard sell, imparting a message that hits almost invisibly. Faced with an ad for fudge cake, say, the brain forgoes the alarm "319 calories! . . . fat alert!" and instead hums, "Yummm . . . must have chocolate."

If, as Vladimir Lenin said, "The right words are worth a hundred regiments," the wrong words can be worth nary a brass button, as when they arrange themselves into a stew like this, from the label on a Spanish red wine: ". . . a good cloak, clean and brilliant with reflexes of medium evolution that show tiles. It has aromas of breeding, prevailing new wood over an elegant and perfumed bottom of spices, and matured black fruits well united and with balsamic memories. . . . It is large in retronasal."

Okay, that's not fair; perhaps the translator was asleep, or had overindulged in balsamic memories. But there's plenty of writing that's odd enough to raise an eyebrow. Consider Kemps Northwoods Classics ice cream, with "Flavors inspired by the Great North Woods." What, a *Consumer Reports* reader asked, does this product taste like? Pine needles? Campfire smoke? Fried walleyes? A canister vacuum cleaner had "full power . . . cleans upstairs and downstairs." A bleach bragged "same inert ingredients as National Brands!"

An ad for loudspeakers said that Polk's has been "officially and exclusively authorized by the U.S. Government to call itself 'The Speaker Specialists.' " In other words, the slogan was trademarked. And an ad said Lewmar was "the winch that won the America's Cup" because it was used on the fastest boat. The copy went on to note that the runner-up and many semifinalists had Lewmars, too. So the winch that won the cup also lost it.

Taste "genuine imitation Vermont maple syrup" and "Remember El Paco will never substitute Quality for Price." Ponder the "12 Delicious Ingredients" in Durkee Dailey Crispy Sweet Relish (they included alum and polysorbate 80).

Sometimes the copy is so tasteless, tactless, or just plain tacky, you have to wonder what the writer was thinking. "Have you ever seen a Dead Donkey?" queried an ad in the *London Daily Mail* in 1900. "Good sauces are just as rare." Joseph J. Seldin, author of *The Golden Fleece,* recounts the tale of an undertaker who sent a message to sickly local men: "Dear Sir, having positive proof that you are rapidly approaching Death's gate, I have, therefore, thought it not imprudent to call your attention to the enclosed advertisement of my abundant stock of ready-made coffins, and desire to make the suggestion that you signify to your friends a wish for the purchase of your burial outfit at my establishment."

In Taiwan in 1999, posters on buses and in subway stations advertised a German-made heater. They showed a caricature of Adolf Hitler smiling, wearing a khaki uniform and jackboots, and extending his right arm. "Declare war on the cold front," the ads urged. They were pulled.

Who writes this stuff? As of 1999, there were 13,833 advertising agencies in the United States, with 153,124 employees. The first employee in American retailing to write ad copy full-time is said to have been John E. Powers, hired in 1880 to write ads for John Wanamaker's department store. He was of the disarmingly candid school of copywriting. In fact, it seems he often told the truth. "The price is monstrous," he wrote of one item. "Look better than they are, but worth a quarter (25 cents), we guess," he wrote of others.

Novelists and poets including Sherwood Anderson, Stephen Vincent Benét, John P. Marquand, and Joseph Heller found the copywriter's life financially rewarding from time to time. For an Iowa laundry, F. Scott Fitzgerald composed the slogan: "We keep you clean in Muscatine." So the agitator beats on, floating against the current, borne back ceaselessly into the spin cycle.

Do copywriters really get juiced about the products they praise? Helen Woodward, one of the highest-paid adwomen in the early twentieth century, wrote of the need for "a passion for converting the other fellow, even if it is to something you don't believe in yourself." She supposed she might someday have a canned soup to advertise. The idea of selling soup would bore her, she realized, until she looked into the specific product. Then she would be excited at the thought of persuading millions to eat it. Once the romance was over, nothing would induce her to eat the soup, no matter how good it was.

In the early 1930s, after ads began featuring photos, copywriters were said to be an endangered species. One wag described the remaining responsibilities of the copywriter as filling in the space under the words "A Suitable Caption Goes Here." Nevertheless, "creatives" are still with us. Given the five-word definition of an advertising employee coined by Lee Bristol, a founder of Bristol-Meyers—"Yes, sir! No, sir! Ulcer!"—perhaps we should end with a small huzzah for a piece of truly effective ad copy. (The tale that follows has been attributed to Mark Twain, but despite the reference to his boyhood home, its authorship is hard to confirm.)

Once upon a time, a man made a habit of sitting outside a hotel in Hannibal, Missouri, and reading the newspaper. One day, he spotted a small patent-medicine ad that read: "Cut this out. It may save your life." The man dutifully clipped the ad and kept reading, but as he glanced through the hole he had made, he saw an enemy holding a knife and sneaking up on him. The man dropped the paper, grabbed a chair, and knocked out his would-be attacker. > > >

Not exactly Mr. Rogers' neighborhood

Call us crazy, but our celebrations don't usually involve gunfire. (If they did, it would take something a lot stronger than bulletproof glassware to make us carefree.)

—*September 1999*

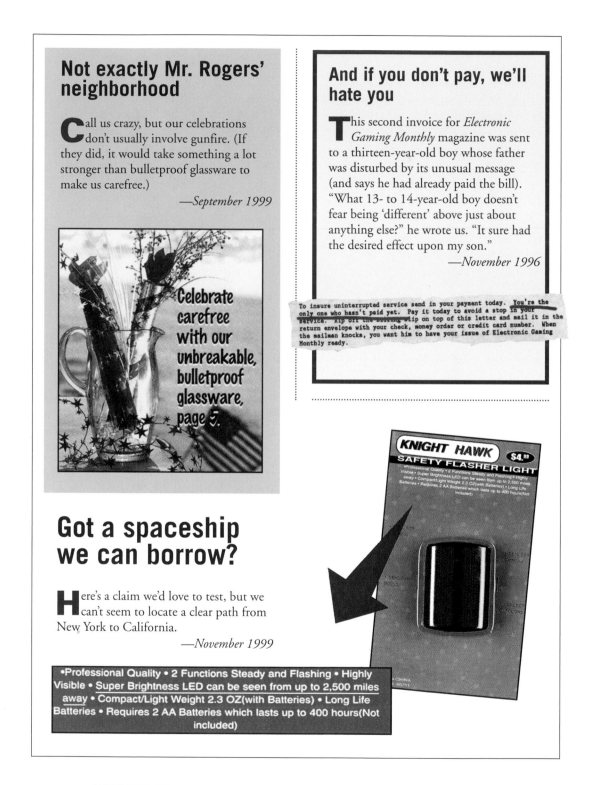

Celebrate carefree with our unbreakable, bulletproof glassware, page 5.

And if you don't pay, we'll hate you

This second invoice for *Electronic Gaming Monthly* magazine was sent to a thirteen-year-old boy whose father was disturbed by its unusual message (and says he had already paid the bill). "What 13- to 14-year-old boy doesn't fear being 'different' above just about anything else?" he wrote us. "It sure had the desired effect upon my son."

—*November 1996*

To insure uninterrupted service send in your payment today. You're the only one who hasn't paid yet. Pay it today to avoid a stop in your service. Rip off the mailing slip on top of this letter and mail it in the return envelope with your check, money order or credit card number. When the mailman knocks, you want him to have your issue of Electronic Gaming Monthly ready.

Got a spaceship we can borrow?

Here's a claim we'd love to test, but we can't seem to locate a clear path from New York to California.

—*November 1999*

KNIGHT HAWK $4.⁹⁹
SAFETY FLASHER LIGHT

•Professional Quality • 2 Functions Steady and Flashing • Highly Visible • Super Brightness LED can be seen from up to 2,500 miles away • Compact/Light Weight 2.3 OZ(with Batteries) • Long Life Batteries • Requires 2 AA Batteries which lasts up to 400 hours(Not included)

Duh!

A Minnesota reader was amused at the boast on a package of videotape storage cases he bought. "I tested the cases," he writes, "and found this to be true. What surprised me is the fact that the cases also automatically become stationary when set down."

—August 1999

EACH STORAGE CASE AUTOMATICALLY BECOMES PORTABLE WHEN CARRIED

Gee! So are knives, pencils, apples, T-shirts . . .

T he circled message comes courtesy of Sanyo Products, which helpfully tells visitors to its web site that its cordless can opener, toaster oven, and salt-and-pepper mill are also Y2K compliant.

—June 1999

PACK YOUR BAGS
Helps make under eye lines, puffs, circles and shadows. All About Eyes $25

They're charging $25?

H ey, most people get those things free!

—May 1999

Water, water, everywhere

A puzzled Massachusetts reader sent us this label from the front of a jug of Miscoe Spring Natural Spring Water. "Several hundred years ago," a second label notes, "the Nipmuck Indians discovered a hidden spring with water so pure, clean, and naturally refreshing, they believed it held special powers. They called it Miscoe. Today you can drink from this very same spring." But the front label says the "Spring Water Source" is Somers, Connecticut, and Wilton, New Hampshire. "This must be a very large spring," we observed to a gentleman in the lab at Garelick Farms, the company that bottles the water. His explanation: There is a Miscoe Spring in Massachusetts, but its supply doesn't keep up with demand, so the company also takes water from springs in Somers and Wilton. We didn't ask whether the Nipmuck had been there, too.

—July 1997

The Ice Age comes to Florida

Is it crazy to assume that Glacier Springs Drinking Water, its label adorned with an icy mountain range, might come from a glacial spring? Guess so. Small type reveals that the water has been subjected to reverse osmosis, carbon filtration, and various other treatments and that it bubbled up not from the arctic tundra but from (drum roll here) Miami's municipal water supply.

—May 1999

What's in a name?

A Maryland reader was amused, as were we, by the first instruction for this Kingsford Table Top Charcoal Grill.
—October 1999

TABLE TOP CHARCOAL GRILL
ASSEMBLY INSTRUCTIONS

MODEL NUMBER: B-1486

DO NOT PLACE ON TOP OF ANY TABLE
N'UTILISEZ PAS CET APPAREIL SUR QUELQUE SURFACE DE TABLE
NO UTILICE EL APARATO SOBRE CUALQUIER SUPERFICIE DE LAS MESAS

A gallery of goofs

1. A possible translation: Go ahead and use your mind to bend a spoon, but thinking hard won't make this pan last any longer.

2. This Olde World painter seems to have forgotten the company's No. 1 secret to a long-lasting paint job.

3. Guess the illustrator got tired after six slats.

—October 1998

❶

SILVER NON-STICK
12" STIR FRY PAN

DO NOT USE MENTAL TOOLS FOR PROLONGING THE LIFE OF THE PAN

❸

8 Slat Wooden Park Bench

18⁸⁸

With Cast Iron Frame!

Other Stores Want $29.99!

❷

Olde World Painting's "4" secrets to a long lasting high quality exterior paint job!

1. "Oil" Based Paints. (Not Latex)
2. 40 Year Warranty, Silicone Based Caulk.
3. Quality Preparation. (Scraping, Sanding and Clean
4. High Quality "Lustre"™ Priming.

Moor[...]
Latex
House Pa[...]

Benjamin M[...]

A counterintuitive pair

1. Note the caveat for the Duracraft "window fan." The owner's manual goes on to give detailed instructions for installing the fan you-know-where.

2. The directions say not to use the M-X-Treme 4 in-ear headphones while cycling. And that guy on the front of the package is . . . walking?

—*March 1999*

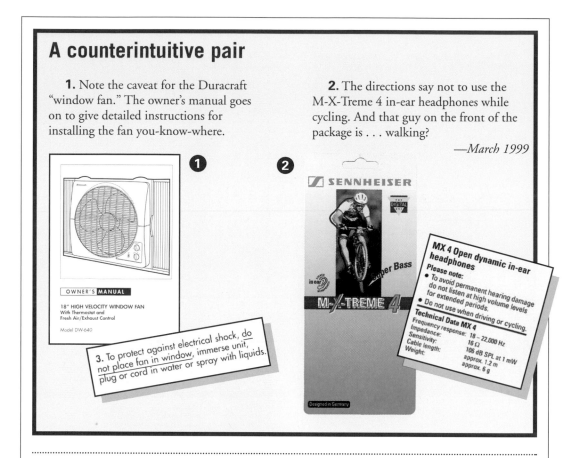

OWNER'S MANUAL

18" HIGH VELOCITY WINDOW FAN
With Thermostat and
Fresh Air/Exhaust Control

Model DW-640

3. To protect against electrical shock, do not place fan in window, immerse unit, plug or cord in water or spray with liquids.

SENNHEISER

super Bass

M-X-TREME 4

Designed in Germany

MX 4 Open dynamic in-ear headphones

Please note:
• To avoid permanent hearing damage do not listen at high volume levels for extended periods.
• Do not use when driving or cycling.

Technical Data MX 4
Frequency response: 18 – 22,000 Hz
Impedance: 16 Ω
Sensitivity: 106 dB SPL at 1 mW
Cable length: approx. 1.2 m
Weight: approx. 6 g

New.   Old.   30 Minutes Later. Both.

The Krylon® 30-Minute Makeover means anything can really look like something-fast. For an incredible selection of colors, and the fastest drying time for the smoothest finish, there's Krylon. The no runs, no drips, no errors™ spray paint. Call 1-800-4-KRYLON.

KRYLON

© 1998 Sherwin-Williams Diversified Brands, Inc.

You and who else?

Copy accompanying this ad for Sherwin-Williams Krylon suggests you "turn an old end table into something great in about half an hour." How? As the copy explains, you just remove all hardware, strip and scrape off the old paint, sand, wipe, prime, sand again, mask areas you don't want painted, and apply two coats of paint.

—*December 1998*

What to do on Monday

A reader sent us the washing instructions for a gym outfit she'd had to buy for her daughter's school show. The Elite Gym-King garment ("Made with care in the USA") was not guaranteed unless the special instructions were strictly adhered to: "Machine wash only in COLD water. . . . DO NOT WASH with any other garments. . . . Do not wash more than 1 garment at a time. . . . Do not wash by hand or in a small volume of water. Use large load water level. Immediately after rinse cycle remove garment and machine dry. Do not leave in washer for any length of time. DO NOT HANG OR LAY OUT TO DRY."

—*September 1990*

Easier said than done

E very now and then we stumble across a package instruction that leaves us scratching our head—or raising our eyebrows. Three cases in point:

Once you've read the instructions on a box of Pepperidge Farm frozen raspberry turnovers, it's too late to obey them: "Preheat oven to 475°F before taking package from the freezer."

A New Jersey reader was surprised to read the "patient counseling" instructions a local pharmacist typed onto a recent prescription for her cat. "Do not mix with alcohol," it warned. "Use caution when

Waxing not on the wane

W hew! Was a North Carolina reader glad after she had finished waxing her car with Nu Finish, "the once a year car polish." She wouldn't have to do that job, which took her several hours, for another year. She was less happy when she came to the very last small direction on the flip side of the bottle: "For maximum protection, apply second coat in 30 days."

—*February 1997*

driving or operating machinery." Our reader noted, "We had no idea what the cat was up to when he felt good!"

But the real eye-opener comes from Japanese manufacturer Yamaha. While perusing the assembly instructions for his new Electric Grand keyboard, a reader found a diagram showing assorted pieces of hardware and labeled with a single Anglo-Saxon word of instruction. We can't repeat the instruction, but we believe the company meant "screw."

—*August 1993*

You mean they're not glued down?

Translation: Take the cookies out before you heat the meal.

—November 1998

Quick, somebody tell the Earth

According to the fine print, Fridays now end at nine P.M., and Saturdays and Sundays last eleven hours.

—July 1998

Huh?

You never know when the spark plugs on that toilet are going to give out.
—*May 1998*

- - COUPON $AVER - -

TOILET TUNE-UP

1st Toilet

$**89**

2nd Toilet

$**59**

3rd Toilet

$**54**

Expires 12-2-97

Timber!

The lonely line of type on this AT&T bill says, "You have chosen to receive the environmental bill format to save paper."
—*October 1997*

A bare-bones guarantee

Eastpak uses this label to tout its backpack's "lifetime guarantee." Despite the implication that the pack has outlived its owner, the guarantee, like many others, is for the lifetime of the product, not the owner. Moreover, Eastpak's guarantee doesn't cover "normal wear and tear." So the pack will probably last until it wears out.
—*November 1997*

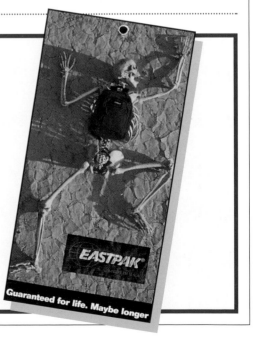

EASTPAK

Guaranteed for life. Maybe longer

What's teh word?

Yeah. You won't have any hassels/has-tles/hasles . . . problems when your spell checker works to prefection. (The typos come courtesy of an Egghead Software catalog and an ad for the software program Newsletters & More.)

—September 1996

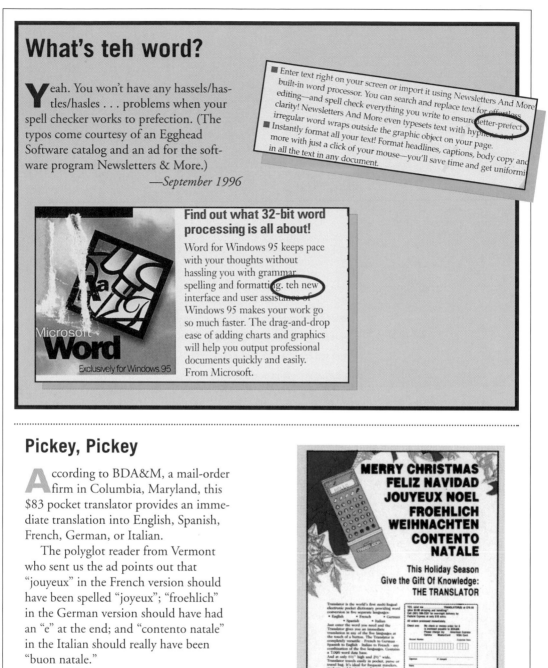

■ Enter text right on your screen or import it using Newsletters And More built-in word processor. You can search and replace text for effortless editing—and spell check everything you write to ensure letter-prefect clarity! Newsletters And More even typesets text with hyphens and irregular word wraps outside the graphic object on your page.
■ Instantly format all your text! Format headlines, captions, body copy and more with just a click of your mouse—you'll save time and get uniformi in all the text in any document.

Find out what 32-bit word processing is all about!

Word for Windows 95 keeps pace with your thoughts without hassling you with grammar, spelling and formatting. teh new interface and user assistance of Windows 95 makes your work go so much faster. The drag-and-drop ease of adding charts and graphics will help you output professional documents quickly and easily. From Microsoft.

Microsoft
Word
Exclusively for Windows 95

Pickey, Pickey

According to BDA&M, a mail-order firm in Columbia, Maryland, this $83 pocket translator provides an immediate translation into English, Spanish, French, German, or Italian.

The polyglot reader from Vermont who sent us the ad points out that "jouyeux" in the French version should have been spelled "joyeux"; "froehlich" in the German version should have had an "e" at the end; and "contento natale" in the Italian should really have been "buon natale."

We hope the electric translator is smarter than the ad copywriter.

—May 1990

Calling all contortionists

Ameritech VoiceSelect, a cellular phone feature, lets you dial without lifting a finger, the ad points out. But the ad goes on to say that you "press two buttons, say the name of the person or number you'd like to call, and VoiceSelect takes care of the rest." Maybe you press those two buttons with your elbow.

—September 1996

And the type is for typographical purposes

We're *still* trying to figure out what Wickes furniture stores meant by the note it printed in an ad last summer.

—April 1996

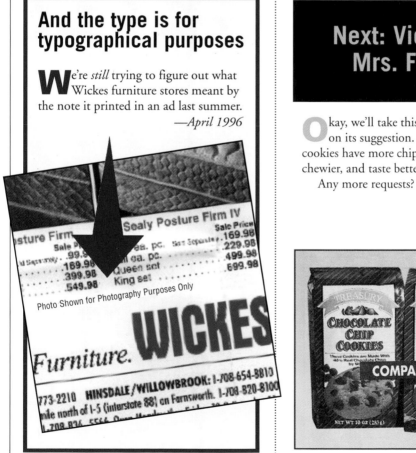

Next: Vicks vs. Mrs. Fields

Okay, we'll take this drugstore ad up on its suggestion. We think the cookies have more chips or raisins, are chewier, and taste better than Benadryl. Any more requests?

—March 1996

I guess we could, like, watch the ash form

Incense (noun): Material used to produce a fragrant odor when burned.

—*January 1996*

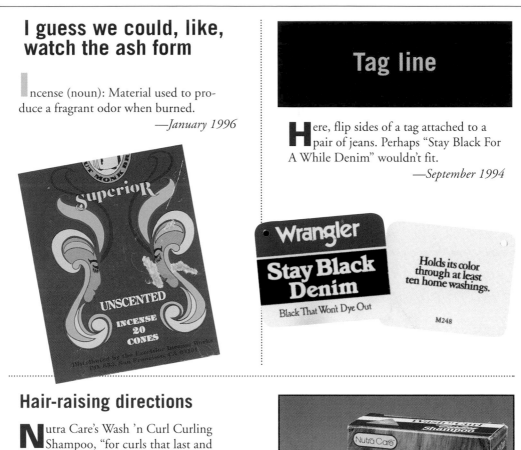

Tag line

Here, flip sides of a tag attached to a pair of jeans. Perhaps "Stay Black For A While Denim" wouldn't fit.

—*September 1994*

Hair-raising directions

Nutra Care's Wash 'n Curl Curling Shampoo, "for curls that last and last," is "formulated with special curl enhancers and volumizers for creating and strengthening curls." You might conclude, as a New Jersey reader did, that it will curl your hair. Not on its own it won't, as she discovered when she read the directions. The shampooer is told to set her freshly washed hair in rollers or to do the following: place head down; dry scalp until the roots of hair are almost dry; return head to upright position; take sections of hair, smooth them around spiral hair brush, and blow dry; then work sections of hair into place by fluffing then with fingers so as not to pull out curls.

—*November 1995*

Floats, too

A Missouri reader spotted this wastebasket ad in a catalog from Viking Office Products of Los Angeles. Noiseless, rustproof, easy to clean, resists chemicals, lightweight, won't chip, dent, peel, or leak. And it has that novel rectangular shape to boot. "What is that new synthetic material?" we wondered. "Sturdy plastic," explained a sales clerk we phoned. Which means, of course, it's also microwaveable—something you can't say about those noisy, rust-prone metal wastebaskets.

—October 1993

That's *Puerto Rico*

P ublishers Choice Video provides "specific details" about real estate, shopping, vacation deals, and natural wonders in Costa Rica, which is described in this ad as a "scenic, secure island," a "friendly, welcoming island," and a "law-abiding island paradise." Whoops. Seems Publishers Choice missed one fact. Costa Rica is not an island.

—January 1996

Quick, fetch the bloodhounds

Employees at a Colorado company found copies of this preaddressed, postage-paid postcard, from Lifestyles Singles Club, on their car windshields recently. Those who didn't appreciate the adornment mailed their card back without filling it out, thus sticking Lifestyles with the postage. But one recipient, intrigued by a warning on the card's flip side, sent her card to us instead. The message: "Mailers of blank cards will be prosecuted."

—*December 1995*

Single??
Register For Free Drawing
No Obligation
VAIL SKI TRIP — LAS VEGAS WEEKEND
$5000 ART COLLECTION or COLOR T.V.
and CLUB MEMBERSHIP
Sponsored by: Lifestyles Singles Club
A Great Singles Club — Fun Dating and Activities
"The Place To Be In Denver"
ll out and send within 7 days — No Stamp Necessary

_____ City _____
_____ Years _____ State _____ Age
s ____No   Phone: Work _____ Zip
rmation about Lifestyles Ltd.: _____ Months
n on how to make extra money ___Yes ___No Home ____
                                ___Yes ___No

1

Taken to the cleaners

A confused—and annoyed—reader sent us a fabric-care tag that had been attached to an item ordered from the J.C. Penney catalog. "100% Cotton Exclusive of Ornamentation," the tag said. "DRY CLEAN ONLY." Why the annoyance? The tag was on a shower curtain.

—*November 1995*

TV or not TV?

The words "as seen on TV" are puzzling enough: Does the ability to pay for a television ad make for a good product? Now, from Carol Wright Gifts, comes this even stranger boast. What's next, "kind of like the ones that are similar to those seen on TV"?

—*October 1995*

You don't say

And if we're not 100% pleased, we will, too.

—October 1995

Long hot summer

Wow—more than 26 percent of home burglaries take place between Memorial Day and Labor Day, says this ad from ADT Security Systems. What the ad fails to mention is that more than 26 percent of the year also takes place between those dates (26.6 percent, to be exact).

—September 1995

Heartbreak hotel

We can only hope that two lonely souls in neighboring suites will find each other.

—September 1995

Hey, whatever

This message, apparently from a writer who ran out of steam, appeared on a plastic bag holding a wallet bought by a Michigan reader. The more conventional wording advises people to keep plastic bags away from children because of the danger of suffocation.

—*August 1995*

Out of circulation

Perhaps, a West Virginia reader muses, the heating pad that came with these instructions is to be used by androids only.

—*July 1995*

CAUTION - THIS PAD IS NOT TO BE USED ON OR BY AN INVALID, SLEEPING OR UNCONSCIOUS PERSON, OR A PERSON WITH PRIOR BLOOD CIRCULATION UNLESS CAREFULLY ATTENDED.

Instant karma

We blinked when "previously owned" cars replaced "used" ones; we blinked twice recently when a reader sent us a flyer from National Piano Institute Marketing Services. It announced the sale of pianos that had been loaned to Northwestern University the year before. These year-old loaners weren't "used" or even "previously owned." Apparently, they were reincarnated pianos. The flyer called them "pre-existing."

—*January 1995*

daer ot drah tuB

As a California reader points out, you will need one tool to install this toilet-paper roller: a mirror.

—*July 1995*

NATIONAL
PIANO
INSTITUTE
MARKETING
SERVICES

Oh. So you'll refreeze our pipes?

Perhaps Brown's Certified Welding should have thawed out this wording a little more.

—March 1995

But can Lois twirl a baton?

Flyers from "Miss Junior America: the one and only career-oriented, new lifestyle pageant," arrived in a reader's mail. A letter told Lois Martinez, "You have been recommended for our city queen program by a teacher/student in your school or your dance/modeling/voice instructor. . . .We only consider new applications upon recommendation from established community leaders and upstanding citizens."

Instead of being flattered, our reader was flummoxed. "Lois," she informed us, "is my cat." Despite the fact that the pageant's founding principles include honesty, our reader surmised that Miss Junior America found out about Lois from a mailing list on which the cat's name appears, not from any community leader. After all, our reader said, she has never known the cat to take dance, modeling, or voice lessons or to associate with anyone in the community, upstanding or not.

—September 1994

Miss Junior America

How about the unpopular rectangular size?

A reader from Arkansas expressed doubt that the folks at towel-maker Excello Ltd. excel at geometry.

—September 1994

FLOUR SACK TOWELS
Popular Square Size 29" x 28"

When Rover roams

Our award for Euphemism of the Month goes to Comtrad Industries, maker of Radio Fence, an underground electrical barrier that works with a special collar to keep a dog from straying. Nice idea, but the reader of Comtrad's ad might be puzzled by what happens when the dog disobeys a warning beep and crosses the barrier. The copy repeatedly refers to a "small, electrical correction." Look hard enough and you'll find, once, a definition: The correction is "similar to a [harmless] static electricity charge." Such elaborate phrases to avoid one simple word. We don't know about the dog, but we're shocked.

—August 1994

Enervated bunny

This eighteen-inch Plush Energizer Bunny, available for proofs of purchase from Energizer batteries, comes with "removable drum, mallets, and shoes." But instead of going . . . and going . . . and going, it just sits there. Why? It's not battery-operated.

—May 1994

Gender benders

Every Robin, Kim, and Sandy has probably received a sales pitch addressed to a Robin, Kim, or Sandy of the opposite sex, but sometimes a mistake in gender is harder to understand—and especially infelicitous.

When Playboy wanted to "construct" the perfect woman by describing her brains, life style, work style, and vital statistics, it asked for help from a "a full-blooded male" who represented "The Sophisticated Male Of The Nineties" and had been selected "from the many intelligent men in and around your state." That description surprised a Colorado woman named Victoria, who feared that her idea of female perfection might not be quite what Playboy was looking for.

A different characterization greeted Edward Groth III, a manager in the Technical Division at Consumers Union. He found that a recent missive had not only changed his sex but given him multiple personalities. "The Literary Guild," it said—"the book club for all the women you are."

—June 1994

Error go bragh

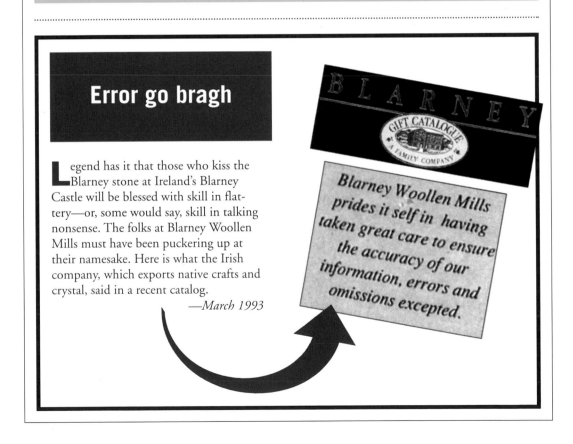

Legend has it that those who kiss the Blarney stone at Ireland's Blarney Castle will be blessed with skill in flattery—or, some would say, skill in talking nonsense. The folks at Blarney Woollen Mills must have been puckering up at their namesake. Here is what the Irish company, which exports native crafts and crystal, said in a recent catalog.

—March 1993

Blarney Woollen Mills prides it self in having taken great care to ensure the accuracy of our information, errors and omissions excepted.

About that hole in the ozone layer. . .

Funny, we remember when blocking a mere 100 percent of the sun's rays was considered an achievement.

—*January 1993*

Coupons are good. No, bad. No, good . . .

Sometimes a slipup affords consumers a peek at marketing strategies of which they would otherwise be unaware. Witness these two flyers for Dash laundry detergent, which appeared the same day in different North Carolina newspapers and seemed to catch Procter & Gamble in the midst of a debate about the merits of coupons.

We asked the company why it provided a coupon for Dash in one paper while boasting elsewhere that Dash comes with no coupons. A company representative explained that the "throw away your coupons" concept was still in development and the ad shouldn't have been published. "We goofed," she said. "You can print that."

—*December 1992*

Mouse-ka-time

This advertisement in a Service Merchandise catalog caught the eye of a West Virginia reader, who suspected Mickey was living in Disney time. Not so, an official in Service Merchandise's watch department assured us: "Mickey says many things, but usually he says the correct time." The official explained that setting display watches (digital or analog) at 10:10 is an industry standard, "but our advertising department clearly didn't look at the product." We bet Bugs would have known the right time. Ha ha. See ya.

—*January 1993*

Speak-you English?

Those little booklets that accompany CDs often provide a wealth of information about the music, the musicians, or the composer. Sometimes, however, a little something gets lost in the translation. Witness the booklet that came with a CD recording of Arthur Honegger's *Le Dit des Jeux du Monde* from Cybelia, a French record company.

We flipped past the French text and on to the English version, hoping to gain some insight into the composer's life and works. We learned that Honegger "should have written for makeshift orchestra or heterogeneous instrument, sometimes invented, which has been called odd-jobs which can play a stimulate function for musicale imagination and for artistic evolution."

We learned, too, that "An other lyric testimony of the composer particulary touching because he answers to a demonstrative wager."

The booklet calls the seventh number on the CD, "Les Hommes et la Terre," a work "as fascinating as jail door" and mentions in passing a Belgian musicologist who is "now disappeared."

But surely the most noteworthy bit of intelligence we gleaned is that "Schoenberg's name has been said several times like a scarecrow for this work!"

—*August 1992*

Hello, Central, get me 18005551696034858369394163859050488765987 6

"Great news," begins a letter announcing Value Phone, a deal between Discover Card and Sprint to enable card holders to use their credit card when making long-distance telephone calls. Combination credit/phone cards aren't new: AT&T's Universal card and MCI's Visaphone card have been around for a couple of years. Nevertheless, we marveled at the announcement's claim that "Calling with your card is easy."

To make a long-distance call, the letter explains, all you need do is dial

Sprint's 11-digit access number. Then 0. Then the 16-digit account number from your Discover Card. Then a four-digit "Personal Access Code." As our Staffer Who Counts Things determined, that's 42 digits. MCI's Visaphone card works similarly, but AT&T's Universal card enjoys a small advantage: With it, you punch only 25 digits.

Our staffer also commented that it's no mean feat to hold a receiver in one hand and a card in the other while tapping phone buttons 42 times with your pinky.

—*August 1992*

Negatively believable

A tag from Duracraft electric fan brags that it is "Manually Reversible." So you can reverse the flow of air by flipping a switch? No. "Manually reversible" means you can pick the fan up and turn it around.

—October 1991

Model DB-10
10" Box Fan with SAFEGUARD™ Child Resistant Switch
Powerful 2 Speed Motor
Manually Reversible
Use it Anywhere -
On a Table or in a Window
1 Year Limited Warranty

What does it do?

A reader from New York city declared this label, from a plastic cutting board, worthy of a "Disclaimer Hall of Fame."

—June 1991

KING
KING **CUTTING BOARD®**

DISCLAIMER
Manufacturer has made no affirmation of fact and has made no promise relating to this plastic sheet which has become any basis of a sale or transaction which has created or amounted to an express or implied warranty that this sheet would conform to any affirmation or promise, and disclaims any warranty of merchantability or fitness of this sheet for any particular purpose whatsoever.

A lawyer's dream?

W hen he applied for a $5 rebate for "using" Rubber Queen floor mats earlier this year, a Massachusetts reader had no idea he was initiating litigation.

—October 1999

Rubber Queen

THE LEADER IN AUTOMOTIVE MATS AND ACCESSORIES
Thank you for suing Lancaster!

Forget something, sir?

S tein Mart, a clothing store in Richmond, Virginia, recently advertised a sale featuring "A complete wardrobe for men . . . Under $100!"

Stein Mart's complete wardrobe consisted of a blazer, shirt, tie, and belt. But, as the reader who sent us the clipping asked, shouldn't a gentleman's wardrobe include trousers? The belt would look funny without them.

—May 1992

WARDROBE **SALE**
SAT. & SUN. ONLY!
A COMPLETE WARDROBE FOR MEN...
UNDER $100!

▶ CLASSIC BLAZER
▶ DRESS SHIRT
▶ SILK TIES
▶ LEATHER BELTS

PICTURE THIS

CHAPTER 3

"Regrettably, advertising can sink much lower visually than verbally. . . . It's one thing to listen to a comedian imploring you to buy a toothpaste . . . but to see him looking at you, sincerity shining in his eyes—well, one has to be steeled to that."

Consumer Reports, May 1947

Copywriters weren't put out of business by illustrators and photographers after all, but you may need to look no farther than the bedroom closet (home of the Nike swoosh) or the liquor cabinet (home of Absolut vodka) to realize how far images have climbed into our lives. Images sell on an emotional, not cerebral, level; they can be more quickly grasped than words yet convey an equally complex message; and they can arouse less psychological resistance. Marshall McLuhan was probably not the first to note that people lack the ability to argue with pictures.

Let's put images aside and listen to the words of one well-known TV ad.

MAN #1: Hey, cookies! Say, you know I think our neighbor might like one, too.
GIRL: There you go.
MAN #2: Thank you. Delicious.
MAN #1: Terrific! Excellent!
ANNOUNCER: Got milk?

What the words leave for the images to say is that (1) the setting is a hospital room where a patient is receiving visitors who have brought chocolate-chip cookies; (2) the "neighbor" is the guy in the next bed; (3) that guy is wrapped like a mummy—totally immobilized, in a cast from head to toe; (4) when the mummy swallows the cookie the visitors have offered through a small hole in his head cast, he starts choking; and (5) he's left with a horrified look in his eyes, unable to tell the visitors that he needs a swig of the milk they're drinking.

Early advertisers were aware of the power of pictures. Montgomery Ward, a traveling salesman for a Chicago dry-goods store, published the first mail-order catalog and discovered that sales rose if he enlivened the text with a woodcut. Nineteenth-century ad images were fairly simple hand-drawn wood or steel engravings reproduced in black-and-white. Jumbo the elephant advertised Barnum's Great Roman Hippodrome. A swooning woman appeared in an ad for Dr. Kinman's Heart Tablets. A man with a goatee sold Clark Stanley's Snake Oil Liniment.

As printing techniques grew more sophisticated, advertising images did, too. They became colorful and beautiful, and famous people agreed to create them for lots of money. Among the artists whose work appeared in ads were Frederic Remington, Maxfield Parrish, N. C. Wyeth, James Thurber, Ansel Adams, and Andy Warhol. Sometimes the artist even became the subject. In an ad for Mennen Shaving Cream, Norman Rockwell was shown before an easel. His claim: "I can put more *chuckles* in my pictures when I've had this COOL shave." (One wonders what Rembrandt might have accomplished sans stubble.) James Montgomery Flagg, whose Uncle Sam starred in the "I Want You" posters, flacked for Miller Tires. "Now I have found beauty in Tires," he said. Another illustrator, famed in her time, is now better known for her role as a mom. Maud Humphrey, who illustrated ads and ad premiums for Procter & Gamble and Ivory Soap, gave birth to Humphrey Bogart.

Eventually, ad folk realized that pictures can mess with your emotions in ways that would embarrass a writer. As author Roland Marchand has pointed out, "No advertiser would have dared to present his product under the headline 'God endorses.' But a well-placed, radiant beam of light from a mysterious heavenly source might create a virtual halo around the advertised object without provoking the reader into outrage at the advertiser's presumption."

Cars sailed through the heavens as boys worshiped them with outstretched arms. Warm, smiling, soft-focus families lounged at home next to their new radio in a fashion that would have been saccharine if captioned. Huge refrigerators loomed over tiny towns, inspiring awe; or stood before an audience of neighbors who had pulled up chairs and sat gazing at the appliance with admiration. (In later years, one refrigerator maker discovered a technique that *didn't* work. To sell a defrosting system, the company pictured the refrigerator unattended and with its door wide open. The maker's message was lost on many potential buyers, who thought only of wasted energy and spoiling food.)

Subjects that have proved effective for ages include children, animals, George Washington, and attractive, semiclothed people. At first, semiclothed people were shown only in part or were unattainable: Patent medicine ads were accompanied by heads of beautiful women, but not their bodies; Quaker Oats came close to unwrapping a whole woman, but the figure the company revealed was a clay model of Ceres, goddess of grain. A breakthrough of sorts came when Allen A Hosiery pictured the back of a woman's legs—a be-still-my-heart moment, for 1925. A decade later, a full-body, side view of a female nude (photographed by Edward Steichen, no less) advertised Woodbury's Facial Soap. Oddly enough, the woman's face was hidden. Males had a somewhat more bizarre journey from dignified to dishabille. Although boys were shown unclothed (from the back), men posed in union suits that were retouched and smoothed over so as to leave *everything* to the imagination.

Another tried-and-true marketing move has been to link a product with a person—either a real one (the company founder or CEO) or a fake (a human mascot). In a sense, this kind of image resulted from the rise of recognizable brands. When the local grocer sold you crackers from a barrel, he or she was the face behind the product, and the two of you had a relationship. Once crackers, pickles, and such were no longer loose in barrels or bins but standardized, packaged, and moved to their assigned spot on shelves, manufacturers found that the brand itself might take the storekeeper's place in the product-consumer relationship.

Consumers of the 1880s became familiar with the bald head and droopy mustache of William L. Douglas, who advertised his own line of mass-produced men's shoes. Later famous faces such as Frank Perdue, Dave Thomas, and Orville Redenbacher might well envy Douglas's popularity: Envelopes addressed with only his picture managed to reach him.

Even the made-up product reps—Betty Crocker, Aunt Jemima, the Breck girl, Mr. Clean—are so familiar that their every face-lift is chronicled in the press. Do Betty's tresses say "matronly" this decade or "hard-driven career woman"? And what's with her blouse?

The editor of "Selling It" had brief personal experience with the power of a human image years ago, while working at *Reader's Digest* in the "No's" department. What's that? It's the destination of sweepstakes entries on which people have checked "No," to indicate they don't want to order merchandise. (Yes, those are kept; you really don't need to order.) The *Digest* was then (and still is) occasionally personified by a fabrication named Carolyn Davis, who signed mailers. A lot of people not only thought she was real; they thought of her as a friend and, along with their "No" ballots, sent her news of their husband's diabetes, their wife's blindness, their friend's bankruptcy, their dog's death. The stories were heartbreaking, but like all virtual spokespeople, Carolyn had no heart to break.

By the end of the 1920s, photos began to appear more often in ads, but they—

and eventually film and video images—weren't always what they seemed. An early manipulated image appeared in an ad for a Hoover vacuum cleaner. It consisted of a triptych of photos showing a child playing in a "64% dirty" room, in a "25% dirty" room, and in a "Hoover clean" room. The difference in dirtiness was due not to Hoover's suction power, but to variations in developing the photograph.

Over the years, the FTC has complained about such misleading images as Flavor Gems that were supposed to make Blue Bonnet margarine taste more like butter (the gems, the FTC noted, were actually magnified drops of a "nonvolatile liquid") and the distortion-free glass used in an ad for Libbey-Owens-Ford/General Motors (the clarity of a car window was demonstrated with the window rolled down).

Rapid Shave got into hot water in the 1960s when a TV commercial showed "sandpaper" being shaved as a voice said, "To prove Rapid Shave's super-moisturizing power, we put it right from the can onto this rough, dry sandpaper. It was apply, soak, and off in a stroke." And lo, there was the razor scraping shaving cream and sand right off. In fact, though, the surface wasn't sandpaper—it was a sheet of Plexiglas on which grains of sand had been sprinkled. And the sand wouldn't have come off in a stroke, absent a big delay in the action: Tests showed that real sandpaper had to be soaked in Rapid Shave for nearly one and a half hours before its sand could be shaved off.

In another ad campaign, an ad agency plopped so many marbles into a bowl of Campbell's vegetable soup that the soup looked chunkier than it was. (In ad parlance, the agency "propped" the soup.) The FTC felt such behavior was mmm-mmm bad, and imposed a settlement in which the company consented to avoid such practices in the future.

In 1990, a Volvo TV ad showed a monster truck driving over a row of cars among which was a Volvo 240 station wagon. Guess which car was not crushed? Guess which car's roof was reinforced with steel beams? Guess which cars' roof supports were weakened? Guess who got in trouble? Right on all counts.

More recently, Dannon performed a bit of photo surgery, though it was legal. For print ads, the company digitized its yogurt into childhood photos of now-famous sports stars. For TV, Dannon hired young actors to play the stars as kids and showed them in apparent "home movies" eating, naturally, Dannon yogurt. When you see Fred Astaire dancing with a vacuum cleaner, as he did in a Dirt Devil commercial, you know your leg has been pulled. But when a video shows a pint-sized Pete Sampras look-alike eating yogurt and growing up to be the real Sampras smashing an overhead, and the screen reads "Coincidence or Dannon?" how are you to know that the old images aren't real? (Dannon noted that the athletes said the depictions were realistic—they really did eat Dannon as kids.)

The FTC says that photographic techniques must not be used to exaggerate, distort, or otherwise misrepresent a product's qualities. Demonstrations must convey accurately only the actual properties of the product, and its features cannot be altered. An ad for corn flakes, for instance, must show the company's corn flakes, even if the ad agency has to go through a hundred boxes to get flawless flakes. Mock-ups are okay only if the real product would be hard to show because of technical limitations, or if the mock-up is not of the product being advertised. (If you're advertising chocolate sauce, you may use fake ice cream underneath.)

Among the little substitutions companies sometimes make:

Shampoos or soap suds instead of a naturally foamy head on beer; mashed potatoes instead of ice cream; glycerine or corn syrup instead of water droplets on an "ice cold" can of soda; wine or colored water instead of coffee; white glue along with milk, on cereal; acrylic cubes instead of ice cubes. Consider the recipe for an apple pie à la mode pictured in a bank ad: Cook up instant mashed potatoes and bake them into a lattice crust; spoon apple baby food into the little squares of the lattice; top with a scoop of corn syrup, confectioners' sugar, and shortening. For steam, combine chemicals to make smoke.

The kind of picture problems that find their way into the "Selling It" column often deal with a package image that bears little relation to the product inside. We've seen package photos that made frozen dinners look positively delectable (well, at least edible). Inside, however, the dinners resembled something the cat left behind after a bout of indigestion. We've seen toaster pastries that looked full of blueberry goo but had a mere smear of filling. We've seen a bag of cookies that showed a finely detailed picture of a cookie. Underneath was this message: "Enclosed cookies are smaller and their surface appearance is different from the illustration."

A volleyball net package showed adults straining to reach the top. Inside was a net whose poles were five-foot-three. You'd find that out only by reading a side panel. A "Giant All-in-One Inflatable Christmas Tree" said 52 inches on the package. Small print revealed that the *circumference* was 52 inches. The tree was 26 inches high.

Here's a proposal for businesspeople reluctant to show their product as it is. Why not avoid confusion by picturing something totally unrelated to the product, as did the maker of Dr. D. Jayne's Alterative, a cure for SCROFULA, Indolent TUMOURS, Dropsical Swellings, CANCER, Syphilitic Affections, Carbuncles, and much more. Did Dr. D picture a kid licking a spoon, a nurse ministering to a sick patient, or a cured invalid kicking aside his crutches? Oh, no. His ad featured two men dressed in waistcoats, tights, and boots and perched at the brink of a towering, jagged, rocky precipice. One of the men clung to a nearby palm tree as the other used a rifle to beat off a pair of tigers. > > >

A shade deceptive

"**S**ince 1986," begins an ad for Hunter Douglas's Duette window shade, "this shade has been yanked up and down 3,154 times." It has also survived robot attacks and a hit by a misguided water balloon, yet the "fabric shows virtually no wear and tear." What is Hunter Douglas's secret to great-looking, long-lasting shades? One of them is revealed in tiny print above the photograph: "Dramatization: While this isn't the actual shade, Duette shades are built to successfully endure far worse punishment."

—September 1993

Macho, macho man

"**O**h sure," says The Sportsman's Guide in this catalog listing for oak boxes, "we let her do most of the decorating, and drop a few little pillows here and there . . . but the bottom line is that we've got to have a place for our stuff." The copy goes on to suggest that men use the boxes to store gun-cleaning tools, knives, game calls, and loose bullets. So why did all this leave a Massachusetts reader amused? The sexist put-down and muscular prose didn't quite jibe with the photos of boxes holding sewing supplies and what looks like a string of pearls. Oh, sure, we let *him* do a little sewing. . . .

—November 1998

Big news

We've heard of dwarf trees, but these "Baby Bloodgood" maples, offered by a nursery in Kansas, must be something to see—provided you've got a microscope.

—November 1996

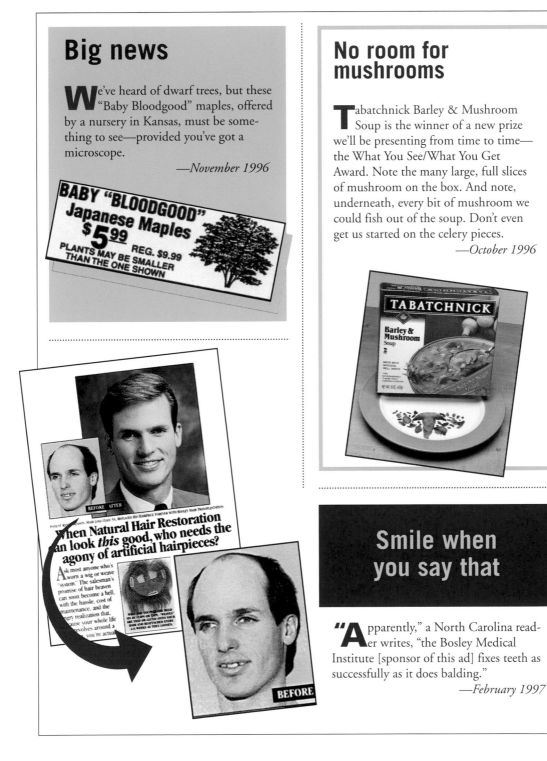

BABY "BLOODGOOD"
Japanese Maples
$5.99 REG. $9.99
PLANTS MAY BE SMALLER
THAN THE ONE SHOWN

No room for mushrooms

Tabatchnick Barley & Mushroom Soup is the winner of a new prize we'll be presenting from time to time— the What You See/What You Get Award. Note the many large, full slices of mushroom on the box. And note, underneath, every bit of mushroom we could fish out of the soup. Don't even get us started on the celery pieces.

—October 1996

When Natural Hair Restoration can look *this* good, who needs the agony of artificial hairpieces?

BEFORE AFTER

BEFORE

Smile when you say that

"Apparently," a North Carolina reader writes, "the Bosley Medical Institute [sponsor of this ad] fixes teeth as successfully as it does balding."

—February 1997

On the other hand . . .

Maybe someone forgot to tell the designer for the Flax Art and Design catalog that this pen is "sculpted to fit in the exact contours" of your, um, *right* hand.

—November 1999

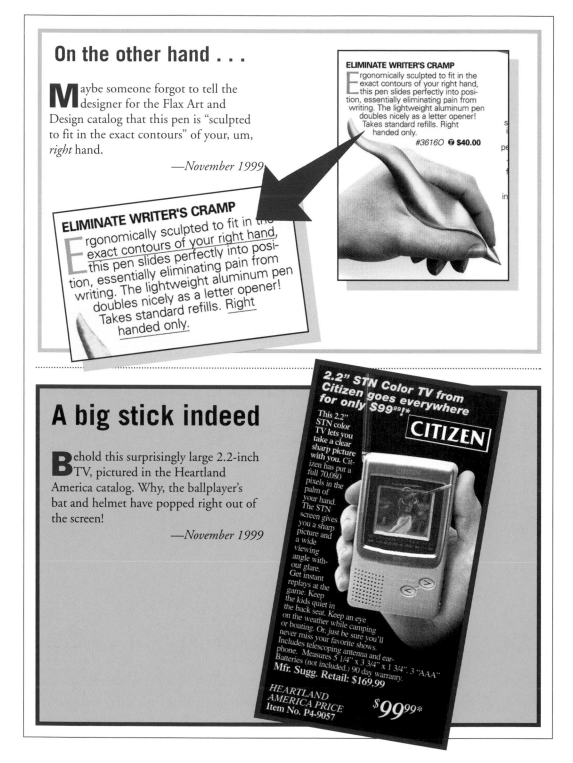

ELIMINATE WRITER'S CRAMP
Ergonomically sculpted to fit in the exact contours of your right hand, this pen slides perfectly into position, essentially eliminating pain from writing. The lightweight aluminum pen doubles nicely as a letter opener! Takes standard refills. Right handed only.
#36160 ☎ **$40.00**

ELIMINATE WRITER'S CRAMP
Ergonomically sculpted to fit in the exact contours of your right hand, this pen slides perfectly into position, essentially eliminating pain from writing. The lightweight aluminum pen doubles nicely as a letter opener! Takes standard refills. Right handed only.

A big stick indeed

Behold this surprisingly large 2.2-inch TV, pictured in the Heartland America catalog. Why, the ballplayer's bat and helmet have popped right out of the screen!

—November 1999

2.2" STN Color TV from Citizen goes everywhere for only $99⁹⁹!*

This 2.2" STN color TV lets you take a clear sharp picture with you. Citizen has put a full 70,080 pixels in the palm of your hand. The STN screen gives you a sharp picture and a wide viewing angle without glare. Get instant replays at the game. Keep the kids quiet in the back seat. Keep an eye on the weather while camping or boating. Or, just be sure you'll never miss your favorite shows. Includes telescoping antenna and earphone. Measures 5 1/4" x 3 3/4" x 1 3/4". 3 "AAA" Batteries (not included.) 90 day warranty.
Mfr. Sugg. Retail: $169.99

CITIZEN

HEARTLAND
AMERICA PRICE
Item No. P4-9057

$99⁹⁹*

A rose by many other names

A sharp-eyed reader from Ohio noticed that this rose has really gotten around—and that it has been renamed, flopped from side to side, and apparently dyed in the meantime. In a 1995 Spring Hill catalog, it was the Queen Elizabeth, a "regal rose" with "masses of large, clear pink flowers." By 1999, Spring Hill was calling it Blue Girl and praising its "deep mauve lavender blooms." Wayside Gardens uses still another name—the more exotic Zepherine Drouhin—but at least the name is consistent from one catalog to another, give or take a vowel here and an accent mark there. On the other hand, Wayside reverses the image and changes the price—its rose is $9.95 in one 1999 catalog and $15.95 in another. Why the difference in price? The customer-service representative wasn't sure. "Maybe it was a different supplier," she noted. Next time, she suggested helpfully, "Buy from the catalog with the lowest price."

—*September 1999*

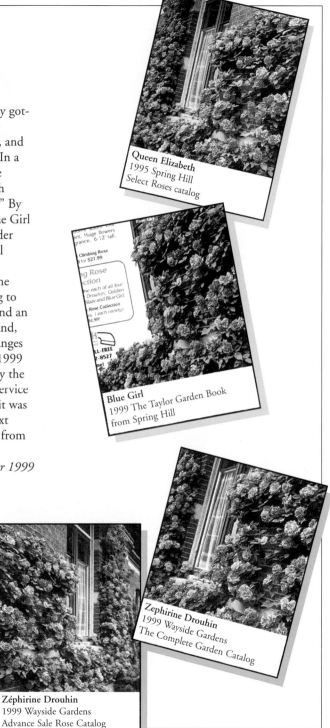

Queen Elizabeth
*1995 Spring Hill
Select Roses catalog*

Blue Girl
*1999 The Taylor Garden Book
from Spring Hill*

Zepherine Drouhin
*1994 Wayside Gardens
The Complete Rose Catalog*

Zéphirine Drouhin
*1999 Wayside Gardens
Advance Sale Rose Catalog*

Zephirine Drouhin
*1999 Wayside Gardens
The Complete Garden Catalog*

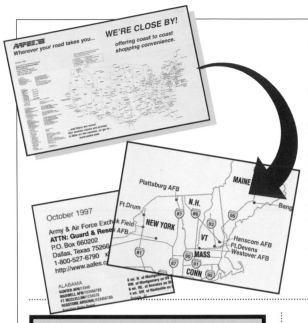

And Normandy is in . . . Belgium?

This map is from the Army & Air Force Exchange Service and lists travel-related services at installations nationwide. Unfortunately, the service confused its coordinates. New Hampshire and Vermont have switched places, and Fort Devens, in Massachusetts, has been placed in the current Vermont—or maybe it's the former New Hampshire. No matter. Although the map is dated October 1997, Fort Devens closed in 1996.

—*August 1998*

I said, "I LOVE YOU!!"

These two ads, a Colorado reader told us, appeared three pages apart in his local newspaper one day last October. Perhaps, the reader suggests, the couple's problem with sexual intimacy stems from the fact that they can't hear each other.

—*May 1998*

Now if you add a new wing . . .

A brochure from Wayne-Dalton Corporation says a new garage door can improve the looks of a house. It's up to the reader to notice that, in addition to a new door, the "after" house has new landscaping, new shutters, a new window box, and a facade-full of sunlight that makes the paint look fresher.

—*May 1998*

Make that "Tree of Darkness"

"**E**legantly light up your home this holiday season with your own Tree of Light," says this Damark catalog, which charges $39.99 for a six-foot tree. However, a key element is not included in the price: lights. You need to use your own, draping them over the snap-together plastic frame as you see fit. No lights? No problem: The catalog will sell you some for an extra $24.99.

—*March 1998*

Whose life is it anyway?

Meet Steve Tyler. And Steve Tyler. The copy under each photograph is identical. It starts with Steve's résumé— "Steve supervises a busy counting lab"— continues with Steve's decision to replace his aging lab system with an ORTEC system, and concludes with the observation that "his evenings and weekends are now delightful. Spent together with his family." So, we asked the company, which one is the real Steve? Neither. "All these people are actors," replied the employee responsible for the ads. Turns out there was supposed to be only one fake Steve Tyler, but the employee preferred the second picture and began using it, too. He ran the ads in different publications—here, *Health Physics* and *Physics Today*—and in different months, but we kind of like them side by side.

—*December 1997*

East is West and West is East

"**A** whole new way of looking at the world," said the envelope that held this brochure for *Compton's Interactive World Atlas.* Well, we guess so: Somalia—the point of land we've indicated—has never been the western tip of Africa before. (The image has been reversed.)

—*December 1997*

Ouch!

"**R**emember when the most important things in life could easily fit in your pocket?" says the front of a brochure from Sharp Electronics Corporation. Inside is this photo of a back pocket holding a couple of smaller brochures for the Wizard Personal Information Organizer. A New York reader saw the literature, bought a Wizard, and was nonplussed to see in the operation manual that although this new important thing in his life could easily fit in his pocket, he might get a sharp pain if he put it there.

—*December 1996*

Clean the unit only with a soft, dry cloth. Do not use solvents.

Do not carry the unit around in your back pocket, as it may break when you sit down. The display is made of glass and is particularly vulnerable.

Replace the batteries as soon as they become weak (see p. 301). Failing to replace weak batteries may result in leakage or lost data.

And now the, uh, Grasshopper?

The Missouri reader who bought Playwell's Sandhopper was taken aback by one precaution listed in the instructions inside: "Do not run toy on sand or immerse it in water."

—*November 1996*

Bigger than life

Notice anything unusual about the piece of map that lies under Optico's magnifying lens? That's right—it's already magnified. But you might not know that until you wrenched the lens from under its plastic bubble.

—*July 1995*

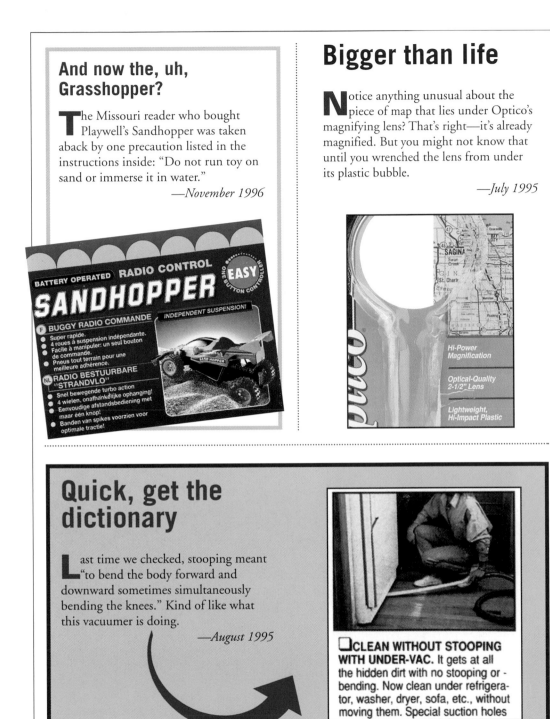

BATTERY OPERATED RADIO CONTROL EASY ONE BUTTON CONTROLLED

SANDHOPPER

INDEPENDENT SUSPENSION!

SAND HOPPER

(F) BUGGY RADIO COMMANDE
- Super rapide.
- 4 roues à suspension indépendante.
- Facile à manipuler: un seul bouton de commande.
- Pneus tout terrain pour une meilleure adhérence.

(NL) RADIO BESTUURBARE "STRANDVLO"
- Snel bewegende turbo action
- 4 wielen, onafhankelijke ophanging!
- Eenvoudige afstandsbediening met maar één knop!
- Banden van spikes voorzien voor optimale tractie!

SAGINA
Swan Creek
St. Charl

Hi-Power Magnification

Optical-Quality 2-1/2" Lens

Lightweight, Hi-Impact Plastic

Quick, get the dictionary

Last time we checked, stooping meant "to bend the body forward and downward sometimes simultaneously bending the knees." Kind of like what this vacuumer is doing.

—*August 1995*

☐CLEAN WITHOUT STOOPING WITH UNDER-VAC. It gets at all the hidden dirt with no stooping or - bending. Now clean under refrigerator, washer, dryer, sofa, etc., without moving them. Special suction holes

Calling Aaron Burr

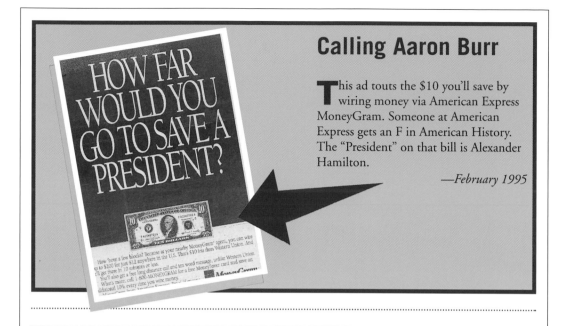

This ad touts the $10 you'll save by wiring money via American Express MoneyGram. Someone at American Express gets an F in American History. The "President" on that bill is Alexander Hamilton.

—*February 1995*

Don't try this at home

We have two new entries for our "Don't kids have enough to worry about?" file. First, the illustration, for Combi International's Avid stroller. That's *carriage* position, folks. (Parents needn't fear; we think any blood shed will be the proofreader's.) Exhibit two: an ad for Fabricland, based in Portland, Oregon. Yes, that bright glow just behind the girls is a sizzling fire.

—*June 1993*

All wet

An Iowa reader strapped on his new Aquatech Sport Watch, "water resistant to 100 feet" (note the surfer on the package) and jumped into a pool. He wasn't worried about the watch, but he should have been—in seconds, its display was blank. Then he looked at the warranty, which said: "This warranty does not cover any failure to function properly due to misuse such as water immersion. . . ."

—*February 1995*

What's wrong with these pictures?

1. Perhaps Kraft Honey Dijon dressing, below, is indeed "A taste that was meant to bee," but a Maryland reader had a waspish comment on Kraft's knowledge of matters apiarian. "Honey from a hornet's nest?" he asked. "Ain't that the bee's knees?"

2. The goal of US Home may be "0 defects, 100% satisfaction," as stated in its brochure, but we still think anyone without a four-wheel-drive vehicle would have trouble getting into the garage. (The house is only a model, the company explained.)

3. Jeep's ad says, "This Jeep Grand Cherokee Is Hundreds of Miles From Civilization. Its Driver, However, Isn't." We have a question. If the Jeep was driven only five miles—as the odometer shows when the ad is full-sized—how did it get from the manufacturing plant to the middle of nowhere?

—*December 1994*

1: Read our advice
2: Ignore our pictures

A Family Fitness Pocket Guide, packaged with Chex cereals, stresses that cyclists should wear bike helmets. Good advice. Maybe these happy riders, pictured next to that recommendation, were on their way to the helmet shop.

—January 1992

And thereby hangs a tail

What's pictured in Fig. 2? No points for guessing a catapult. The drawing is supposed to show how to use a product sold by RAF Trading. The Life Line is a figure-eight harness that slips over a cat's head and around its chest. The illustrator seems to have missed by a whisker, though. A call to the company elicited the response that, no, that thing around the cat's neck is not its tail but the leash. "Quite an accomplishment," one of our readers noted, "having a cat grow its own leash."

—November 1991

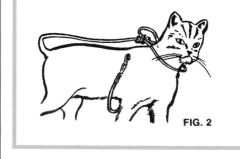

FIG. 2

Vanishing cream

Gone Skin Cream claims to "fade away freckles, ugly skin discolorations, liver spots, age spots and other blotches." Amazingly enough, as an eagle-eyed Colorado reader noticed, it has also erased the shadow under the pointing finger.

—October 1996

Good fences make good sales prospects

A Virginia reader was impressed by the innovative woodwork in this ad for a new town house development near Washington, D.C. It might deter door-to-door salespeople, but wouldn't new homeowners also find fence-jumping a tad inconvenient? An agent for the development assured us that the fence blocks the sidewalk only in front of the model homes. "That's our little sales trick," she disclosed. "People go in a side door and then walk out the front. The fence is a little trap so that we can talk with them when they come out."

—June 1993

Haven't we seen you somewhere before?

W hat a coincidence. When you wear Lipo Slim Briefs (near right), whose "thousands of thermo-active micropore cells produce a gentle massage that destroys deep fat particles," you get exactly the same results as pictured with the Elysée Body Toner (far right), whose "tiniest, gentlest, safest, electronic impulses will make your muscles automatically contract 300 times a minute!"

—January 1997

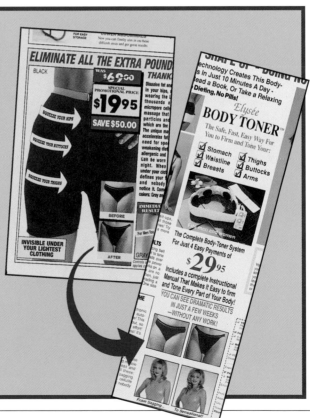

☆ ☆

READY, WORLD?

"Invention, mass manufacture, mass distribution—then slam, bang, hoopla, and the millions roll in."

Sylvia Porter in the *New York Post*
around 1960, writing about cold medicine

According to Mintel's Global New Products Database, U.S. manufacturers introduced 16,460 new products in 2000—everything from ThreeWeed Hair Mud Mask (for dull, tired hair) to Rebound Cool Ice Sports Drink (for dogs). Those wonders joined the likes of Ripped Force Hyperthermogenic beverage, Hey Dude! Steak & Mashed Potato Meals, and Training Treats for Husbands (caramel candies shaped like a dog bone and doled out as a reward for such behavioral modifications as lowering the toilet seat to female-friendly position).

Along with truly different new products come spin-offs from old standbys. Manufacturers have long bought into the French marketing expression "*Cherchez le creneau*" (Look for the gap), and niches are opening up at an alarming rate. In a recent test of detergents, *Consumer Reports* remarked upon the reproductive powers of Tide. At the time, it came in a dozen versions, six liquid and six powder. Each type included a regular nonbleach product with a light scent or a mountain scent, a bleach or bleach-alternative product with a light scent or a mountain scent, a "free" product with no added perfumes or dyes, and a product for front-loading machines.

Certainly advertisers consider "new" a powerful pitch—so powerful that it may bear repetition. A Pontiac was once called not only new but newnew and newnewnew. Still, when a loudly trumpeted "great new!" product is simply a revision, it's tempting to wonder what was wrong with the old "great new!" product. A gum we saw not long ago seems to have found a way to avoid such questions. Its label said, "New! Original Bazooka."

Some manufacturers wish new could go on forever. Maxwell House Instant Coffee was called "A New Coffee Discovery" for many years, and an adman defended the practice: "After all, the New Testament is almost two thousand years old." However, there are limits to newness. First, the FTC says, a product isn't new if it has simply had a face-lift; it must have been reformulated in a material respect related to its performance. Second, everything new must become old. FTC guidelines state that under most circumstances, a product can be new for only six months.

It's the marketer's task to make sure that before they become old, all new products find homes (still, about 80 to 90 percent of new products fail within a year). That means convincing homeowners that they can't live without the new thing, whether it be a safety razor, a computer, a hotel stay, or that mud mask. Aldous Huxley implied that the desire for the new is natural (as can be desire for the old—or, excuse us, olde). In his novel *Antic Hay*, an ad-agency employee discusses a campaign for Gumbril's Patent Small Clothes, trousers lined with air-filled bladders (Gumbril got the idea while sitting in an uncomfortable pew): "People feel superior if they possess something new which their neighbours haven't got. The mere fact of newness is an intoxication. We must encourage that sense of superiority, brew up that intoxication. The most absurd and futile objects can be sold because they're new."

According to another school of thought, people need to be taught to want new products. After all, nearly any new product, absurd and futile or not, could be considered unnecessary at the start—humans had gotten along fine without it for, oh, a hundred thousand years. Ad agency Young & Rubicam once countered that argument in sniffy copy pitching its own services. "Advertising *does* sell people things they don't need," the ad read. "Things like television sets, automobiles, catsup, mattresses, cosmetics, ranges, refrigerators, and so on and on. People really don't *need* these things. People don't really *need* art, music, literature, newspapers, historians, wheels, calendars, philosophy, or, for that matter, critics of advertising, either. All people really need is a cave, a piece of meat and, possibly, a fire."

Point taken, so we'll consider a few inventions that might have left people wondering at the start but that seem to have made them happy over the long haul. How about deodorant? A Cincinnati surgeon invented Odorono in 1907 after he sweated through an operation. Ads wouldn't dare mention the word armpit, but women were able to decipher the headline "Within the Curve of a Woman's Arm," and although some folk said talk of such matters was disgusting, sales took off. (Advertisers left men to sweat for several more years.)

Clarence Birdseye's invention of a way to freeze vegetables yet leave them edible actually helped improve Americans' eating habits. In 1920, the average American ate 110 pounds of vegetables a year. By 1980, thanks largely to freezing, the per-capita consumption of vegetables had doubled.

Before the Scott brothers repackaged tissue paper, sold it for use in bathrooms, and started America on the road toward squeezable Charmin, a "roll" of toilet paper looked like a miniature legal pad.

Not until 1920 could anyone figure out how to surround ice cream with hot chocolate without a messy meltdown. When Iowa schoolteacher Christian Nelson succeeded, he created the Eskimo Pie, and made possible chocolate-coated ice-cream bars to follow.

What about the widely invoked epitome of great new products: mass-produced sliced bread? That's a tricky one. An 1858 ad bragged about the "uniformity" of John Hecker's "Machine-made bread." But sliced bread underwent a shift in image even before the advent of the bread machine. By the 1980s, *Consumer Reports* noted, sliced white bread was "about as chic as polyester."

Sometimes a name itself creates an image that boosts sales. When Baltimore druggist Charles A. Voegeler began selling an all-purpose liniment in the 1800s, he called it Keller's Roman Liniment, put a picture of Julius Caesar on the label, and asserted that Caesar's troops had used it to conquer the world. When that ploy didn't work, he changed the name to St. Jacob's Oil and said the stuff was made by monks in the Black Forest of Germany. It sold well—until Voegeler stopped advertising, at which point his product fell from favor.

Other names sell by bossing buyers. "Uneeda Biscuit" was coined by H. N. McKinney of the Ayer advertising agency. (Rejected suggestions included Wanta Cracker, Taka Cracker, and Hava Cracker.) The product spawned less successful imitators, among them Uwanta beer, Itsagood soup, and *Ureada* magazine.

Sometimes a product succeeds despite its original name. The first Maytag washer with an attached wringer, introduced in 1909, was called "The Hired Girl." William Wrigley, Jr.'s first chewing gums were Vassar and Lotta. The first name for flavored fizzy water was not soda or pop but Phosphate ferrozodone. The zipper found its name only after many false starts, among them "Clasp Locker or Unlocker for Shoes," "Universal Fastener," "C-Curity Placket Fastener," and "Hookless No. 2."

It's always fun to guess which new products will catch the public's favor, and interesting when one launched with great hope—and megabucks—flops. Witness the Edsel. In the 1950s, Ford wanted to make a medium-priced car to which owners of less-expensive Fords could step up—before, presumably, stepping up again to Lincolns. At first, the car was called "E," for experimental car. Ad agency Foote, Cone, & Belding provided sixteen thousand other names within two weeks. Even the poet Marianne Moore was commissioned to come up with suggestions (her most remarkable, Fairfax Cone remembered, was Bullet Cloisonné.) The only name off limits was Edsel, the name of Henry Ford's recently deceased son.

Yet "Edsel" premiered in 1957. People flocked to showrooms, saw the car's front end—later compared to a horse collar, a toilet seat, and an Oldsmobile sucking a lemon—and fled. No amount of positive spin—"Dramatic Edsel Styling is here to stay," "The most beautiful thing that ever happened to horsepower"—made people like the look. No incentives (Ford gave a small model of an Edsel to people who took a test drive) made them buy the car. It was funny-looking, was not fundamentally different from others, was introduced during an economic slump, and was dusted by compact cars like the Rambler. By 1960, the Edsel was history.

Other products we've heard about over the years seem equally misconceived. For those now departed, we say rest in peace. For any extant, we can only ask why. Among them:

- Post's Bran chocolate, called "Bran in candy form."
- Butterfly Art Barbie. Mattel's doll turned forty in 1999, yet one of her personae featured a tattoo on her midriff. (This one's gone: Mattel stopped production after parents complained.)
- Negajinx pendant. This $10 wonder promises "to wipe out your jinxes in 24 hours flat!"
- Vermont Mist: "A nonaerosol spray of pure melted snow & mineral rich water. The best way to moisturize and set your make-up! . . . 4 oz. $4.50." Hard to complain about the price of gas when water is going for 45 cents per sip.
- Breathlight, a combination cigarette lighter and breath freshener.
- The transmission of a personal message "across the cosmos . . . at the speed of light," courtesy of an English firm, for $25.
- An eighteen-karat-gold cat necklace offered in The Fancy Cat Catalog of California for $19,000. Better yet, the matched cat-and-owner pair for $49,000.
- Car-Unlock, a tool that let you break into your car when you locked your keys inside. Of course, you had to remember to take the Car-Unlock with you when you forgot to remove your keys. Then again, perhaps you could have borrowed a Car-Unlock from a thief.

And farewell, for at least a thousand years, to SpaghettiOs 2000, Millenios, Marshmallow Blasted Froot Loops With Millennium 2's, Millenium Energist Revitalizing Emulsion, and Y2K Survival Donuts. > > >

Nice lines, but where's the engine?

A Pennsylvania reader's sons spied the words "Remote Control Caddie" inside the cap of their bottle of Snapple and realized they'd won a prize—a remote-control model of a Cadillac, they surmised. What arrived in the mail several weeks after they submitted a form to claim their prize? The squiggly object at right and a slip of paper. "Simply insert your remote controls in the slots provided," the paper said, "and enjoy hours of movement-free couch-potatoing!"

—*March 1998*

Strikeout

L et's see. According to this ad from the Morgan Mint, baseballs autographed by Joe DiMaggio can cost "hundreds of dollars each," so you're supposed to spend "less than $30" (actually, $29.95 plus postage and handling) for a ball bearing the Yankee Clipper's "authorized facsimile signature." An authorized fake signature? It gets better: The ball comes with a "Certificate of Authenticity." It's an authentic ball, we guess.

—*July 1999*

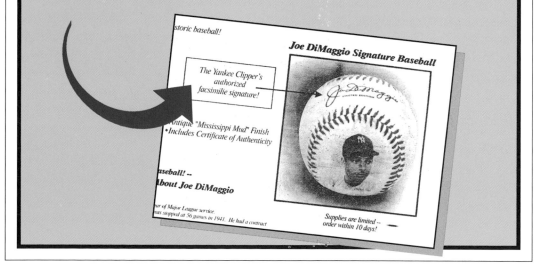

storic baseball!

The Yankee Clipper's *authorized facsimilie signature!*

Joe DiMaggio Signature Baseball

ntique "Mississippi Mud" Finish
•Includes Certificate of Authenticity

seball! --
bout Joe DiMaggio

ar of Major League service.
as stopped at 56 games in 1941. He had a contract

Supplies are limited --
order within 10 days!

Oddball product sighting

With this item, Ohio State fans can presumably eye the Buckeye symbol for eternity.

—*February 1999*

Composite material provides timeless protection.

Enduroglas™... The Strongest Burial Idea In History.

For more information, please call Oak Grove International (800)-462-5476

Budgetel's budget-towel

Use this "guest towel" to clean "just about anything." Okay, we'll use it to wipe our lips. The paper towel is the size of a dinner napkin—and a lot thinner.

—*April 1998*

Guest Towel

WITH OUR COMPLIMENTS
use this towel to clean your...
MAKE-UP
SHOES
LUGGAGE
EYEGLASSES
AUTO WINDSHIELD
RAZOR
OR JUST
ABOUT ANYTHING

Budgetel INNS

Amazing—and true!

This antenna's boasts—it needs no cable box, pulls in all local VHF and UHF channels, requires no satellite fees, and works via "RF technology"—are a tad undermined by the ad's final point. Perhaps the catalog company, Bright Life, thought twice about this revelation: In a later catalog, the last point was missing. For the record, our television expert notes that the antenna has nothing to do with satellites and, at best, would work as rabbit ears do. As for RF (radio frequency) technology, he says, "Every single antenna in the world works that way. That's like saying we all live by breathing."

—*September 1998*

Amazing "Dish" Antenna Works Indoors

• No cable box needed
• Works like any ordinary rabbit ears
• Legal in all 50 states

Only $5

• Gets all local VHF and UHF channels from 2 to 83.
• Works via "RF" technology —pulls signals right out of the air.
• You pay NO satellite fees because you DON'T use satellite signals.
• Not technical razzle-dazzle but a marketing breakthrough.

• Compatible with all TV's

Four score and seven gimmicks ago...

"**T**his fountain pen," says the spring catalog from Fahrney's Pens Inc., "contain the 'genetic essence' of America's greatest president. Using the most advanced technology, a replication of Lincoln's DNA has been crystallized and embedded in the amethyst stone on the crown of each limited edition pen." What in heaven's name could this mean? asked a reader. We asked Fahrney's. "Someone indirectly connected to the company has a patent on being able to recreate DNA from hair," a customer-service representative told us. "Some of Lincoln's hair was saved and passed on in the family." That hair was used to make a copy of Lincoln's DNA, which was stuck atop the pen's cap. The price per pen: $1,650. So, we asked the representative, could someone clone the sixteenth president from your pen? "No, no, no," she replied.

—September 1998

Still crazy

The Wine Enthusiast's Miniature Distilling Machine is "the real thing," the catalog copy states. "Just put in your favorite wine or beer and make great-tasting, full-proof spirits." Or, given what the note says, pay $200 and let it sit on your coffee table.

—January 1998

Yeah, but it's *authentically* fake

Now let's get this straight. The International Millionnaires Society's "authenticated" million-dollar bill (right) is useless as currency; yet it's "a $12.50 Value!"; though you can have it for just $4.95.

Not for you? Then how about the mini Yankee Stadium, complete with a "Certificate of Authenticity" bearing a replica of Yogi Berra's autograph?

—*August 1997*

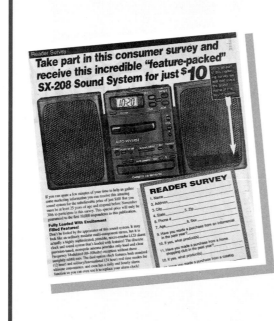

Listen up

Answer questions about your buying habits, this ad says, and you'll receive a "Sound System" for $10. Pictured is a black box with some of the usual sound-system labels. Its base says cassette CD receiver. "It may look like an ordinary modular multi-component stereo," the ad continues, "but it is actually a highly sophisticated, portable, micro-combo LCD alarm clock and sound system that's loaded with features!" The ad goes on to say that "the cleverly simulated CD, cassette, and receiver front panel are so meticulously detailed that it's sure to impress anyone!" In other words, this highly sophisticated sound system is a clock radio.

—*May 1997*

It's also an oven spoon, a stove spoon . . .

Hmm, a microwave spoon. Maybe you leave it in a dish you're "nuking" but need to stir occasionally? Wrong. The small type says, "Not intended for use in microwave." So what does it do? The small type has the answer: "Stirs, mixes and serves."

—April 1996

Could you get more specific?

Just when we were getting used to separate creams for hands, face, and the rest of the body, here comes Estée Lauder Revelation Retexturing Complex For Hands and Chest. As if that target zone isn't narrow enough, the back of the jar shrinks it further. "Apply sparingly with fingertips," it says, "to top of hands and upper chest area." We won't even ask what retexturing is.

—February 1996

Total eclipse

The Franklin Mint's Polyhedral Sundial may be, as the literature states, "precision crafted" and a "most impressive timepiece."

It may be "a spectacular new addition" to "your collection of classic scientific instruments." Its twenty-four separate sundials may be based on an original owned by King Henry VIII that was "designed to simultaneously display the time in various regions throughout the world."

"Each degree marking, minute, and hour line" may "appear in dramatic clarity."

But there's something this $90 timepiece won't do: Since each dial lacks a gnomon, the piece of a sundial that casts a shadow, it won't tell time—anywhere.

—September 1995

Shown approximately actual size of 5¼" (13.3 cm) in height including hardwood base.

A new meaning for "zap"

Under the heading of Things We Never Knew We Needed comes Gunvertor, described by its manufacturer, Ingenius Ideas Inc., as "the world's first universal remote control packaged as a handgun."

Thanks, but we'll stick to tossing popcorn at the shows we don't like.

—September 1994

Reading this will cost you 22 seconds

Here's an entry for the "Thanks for reminding us" award: the Timisis Personal Life Clock, a $99.95 "anti-procrastination tool" from The Sharper Image catalog. When programmed with your age and gender, it displays the number of hours, minutes, and seconds that are statistically likely to remain in your lifetime. (The average person will live a total of 2.4 billion seconds, the catalog points out.) Included in the display are 150 different messages designed to prod you into making the most of the time you have left. For those with more immediate concerns, the Timisis also gives the time of day.

—May 1994

Haven't I seen that face before?

Pictured in the Hammacher Schlemmer catalog is The Recycled Watch, which, the ad copy notes, gives "the environmentally concerned an ingenious way of keeping time." Turns out the $149.95 wristwatch is made from "70% recycled-tin and steel" and comes in a recycled-tin storage box. It doesn't take much ingenuity to question the notion that wearing an ounce or so of recycled steel will help the planet much, or to wonder

whether it isn't just as environmentally correct to save tin by storing a watch on the nightstand. Someone really concerned with husbanding resources might consider a second-hand watch; $149.95 could buy a nice one.

—February 1992

A new meaning for "hair spray"?

"Like getting a new head of hair in just seconds," said the advertisement for 1-Step Cover-Up, a colored spray to cover balding heads.

Would all bald areas—top, back, front, side—really "disappear instantly!"? Would 1-Step really stay on "even in rain!"? Would it thicken our "own natural hair!"?

We paid $9.95 plus shipping and handling for a can of dark brown spray and a bottle of 1-Step shampoo to remove it. One of our chemists told us that the spray consists of propellants, solvents, hair fixatives, hair conditioners, emulsifiers, colorants, and, to put it simply, paint components. On a microscope slide, he pointed out, 1-Step looked like flat barn-brown paint.

To see how the product would look on bald spots, we enlisted two of our follically challenged chemists. Holding the can 6 to 10 inches from their heads, we tried to "protect clothing, skin, and eyes from spray" (although how we were to protect skin when we were spraying scalp was beyond us).

Our guinea pigs, one of whom is pictured, ended up with brown, slightly shiny domes that looked almost naturally thatched—from a distance. Up close, their new hair looked like a paint job. Worse, when we sprayed their heads with water, then dried off, as you might after being caught in a rainstorm, 1-Step turned our towels brown.

Moral: Users should keep an umbrella nearby and other people at arm's length.

—*March 1994*

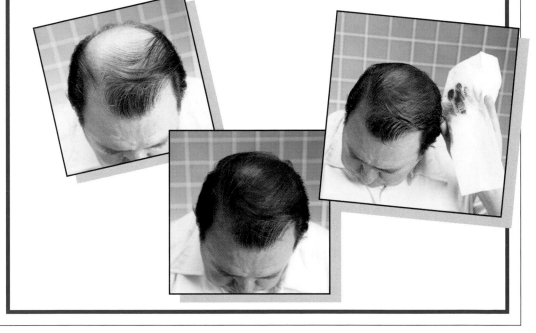

Instant savant

Never had the time or patience to learn a foreign language? No more excuses. We've come across two programs that promise to make the learning process a piece of rice cake, or perhaps gâteau.

From Sony comes Natural Japanese, which offers students a chance to "Learn Japanese in 3 seconds!" Or so proclaims the outside of a brochure for the program. Inside, you'll learn (in thirty seconds or so) that the system is structured around three-second sentences, which students would do well to repeat a few hundred times.

For those who prefer "no effort or memorization on your part," there's the $299 SuperMind Brain Computer from Washington-based Zygon International. "Put on the light-pulse goggles, and head-phones," explains a mailing for the product. Then "push a special button on the command console and an accelerated learning program automatically imprints a complete French lesson onto your brain cells." If that doesn't work, you might want to check out the "smart pills" ped-dled in the same mailing.

—July 1993

Blinds! Cripples! Protects!

"Men—Drop attackers safely with new Liquid-Bullet," begins a recent ad in *TV Guide*. Unlike women's defense sprays ("their dainty vapor can blow in your own face," the ad says), Liquid-Bullet promises a high-powered stream of "the same knockout chemical used by police and military"—tear gas, a Liquid-Bullet Inc. spokeswoman informed us.

"Your attacker's skin feels on fire," the ad says. "He's blinded, fights for breath, helpless for 20 mins." And "unlike MACE, it drops vicious ani-mals." Best of all, claims the ad, Liquid-Bullet "can't injure kids."

Unless, of course, kids manage to unsnap the safety strap and twist the cap to the spray position, in which case kids can spray themselves by mistake.

No permanent problem, the spokes-woman assured us: "At worst, a child would be immobilized for thirty minutes."

—March 1993

Only God can make a tree?

A recent ad reveals that the Christmas tree has evolved in wondrous ways. First there was the real thing, which celebrants decorated themselves. Those trees smelled appropriately firry, but their needles clogged many a vacuum cleaner. Next came imitations with fake needles in pink, silver, even green. They didn't smell the same, but they didn't shed as much, and they could be used year after year.

Now RBM Ltd. has brought us the "most exciting Christmas Lawn Display in our history!" The ad touts the tree as a reproduction of the "Official White House Christmas Tree" and says it's sold fully decorated.

Don't plan on encircling RBM's tree with presents, though. It may tower a full six feet tall, as the copy points out, but it towers "in two dimensions." This tree is made of silk-screened fabric. No smell, no mess, and it rolls up to store in "three inches of space."

—*December 1992*

Derned ferners

The Air Fern, from Sun Bulb Company of Arcadia, Florida, bills itself as a "decorative houseplant that lasts indefinitely out of water or soil." Sound intriguing? The Florida reader who bought one at a local Sears store thought so. The package label explains that the Air Fern, which resembles a plant, is actually a sea animal harvested from the English Channel. What the package doesn't explain is that the "fern" is dried. And dyed. And dead.

When we called the company, an apologetic representative immediately volunteered that the package was misleading, "particularly if you've got the label that says 'As soon as it comes out of the package it bursts into a beautiful bouquet of color.' " The very label we had.

The Sun Bulb representative said the company planned to rewrite the label soon, to make clear that the Air Fern is "just a decorative item," not a living thing.

—*May 1991*

MEDICAL MIRACLES

"For it is a curious truth that we tolerate on the part of sellers what we would deny to beggars—displays in public, however uncouth, of the agonies associated with decayed teeth, indigestion, constipation, dripping noses, acid stomachs, blinding headaches, infected sinuses, ingrown toenails, and itching piles."

Dexter Masters, former director of Consumers Union

The charlatan was born when the first knave met the first fool, Voltaire observed. Knaves seem to have met fools fairly early in the life of the United States, and the meeting more than likely occurred over a bottle of patent medicine. Patent medicines were usually neither sanctioned by a government patent office nor medicinal but called such because in colonial days some bottles bore the king's crest and had a "patent of royal favor." The first successful American patent medicine was Lee's Bilious pills, developed by Dr. Samuel Lee of Windham, Connecticut, sometime before 1796.

Patent medicines played into self-doctoring, a practice still much in vogue, and into a view of the body as a machine that needs to be well oiled. Since only a robot is free from occasional aches or malaise, that strategy worked well.

By 1857, fifteen hundred different patent medicines were being sold in the United States. They jump-started American advertising—and were marketed in newspaper inserts that combined lurid ads with pretend news stories. By the end of the 1800s, patent medicines provided one-third of all profits made by the American press.

What was in those nostrums? One peddler provided a clue: "I can advertise dish water, and sell it, just as well as an article of merit." Good point. According to FDA historian Wallace Janssen, during the 1930s and 1940s thousands of Americans became convinced that "Glyoxylide," promoted by William Koch, M.D., Ph.D., could cure cancer. More than three thousand health practitioners charged patients up to $300 per injection. Yet analysis of the product showed it to be distilled water—cleaner than dishwater, at least.

Water would have been one of the more innocuous concoctions. At best, patent medicines consisted of something that didn't work; maybe harmless roots or herbs. At worst? Sinus powders contained cocaine, syrups were dosed with opium and morphine, painkillers were loaded with toxins, "cures" for cancer were spiced with radium. The medicines were almost always 20 to 40 percent ethyl alcohol, which makers justified as a preservative. It probably did dull plenty of symptoms.

At least one product that called itself snake oil wasn't, really, but the actual stuff wasn't much more appealing. Gerald Carson, who studied the social history of food in America, reported that Clark Stanley's Snake Oil Liniment (a big seller at the Chicago World's Fair, where snakes were killed before the audience's eyes) contained kerosene, camphor, and turpentine.

Among the best-known patent remedies was Lydia Pinkham's. A Quaker from a temperance family in Lynn, Massachusetts, Pinkham began selling in 1875 a remedy she had earlier given to friends. It was eventually promoted as a cure for everything from menstrual cramps to a prolapsed uterus. When her sons figured they could promote it to ease kidney disease, it was sold for that, too. A federal analysis found that it was about 18 percent alcohol plus a soupçon of Jamaica dogwood, pleurisy root, black cohosh, life root, licorice, dandelion, and gentian.

Images of Pinkham in demure Quaker dress appeared everywhere, songs were written about her, and ads spoke of her in the present tense even after her death, prompting one editor to publish an ad next to a photo of her gravestone.

Shortly before World War I, patent medicines faded from favor, driven out of business by the Pure Food and Drug Act and by aspirin, which actually alleviated some of the symptoms the nostrums only claimed to help. Plenty of products lined up to take their place. Even those now better known for other properties have advertised health. In 1915, Listerine was to be used as a scalp rub and baby wash; Coca-Cola was "the ideal brain tonic . . . for headache and exhaustion"; Hires root beer helped "even a cynic to see the brighter side of life"; Quaker Oats built children up symmetrically.

Then there was tobacco, whose drawbacks were evident even in the era of King James I. Its use, he noted, was "a custome Lothsome to the eye, hatefull to the Nose, harmefull to the braine, daungerous to the Lungs, and in the blacke stinking fume thereof, nearest resembling the horrible Stigian smoke of the pit that is bottomelesse."

Once cigarette makers managed to create a smoke people could inhale without coughing, just before World War I, they seemed to think they were making the nearest thing to health food and hired opera stars to testify that tobacco left them in fine voice. Cigarette companies also fired the first salvo in a war against candy with the exhortation, "Reach for a Lucky instead of a sweet." A New York candy store fought back with, "The cigarette will enflame your tonsils, poison with nicotine every organ of your body, and dry up your blood." In the end, a truce was declared, with comical results: Old Gold cigarettes suggested, "Eat a chocolate, light a cigarette—and enjoy both! Two fine and healthful treats."

The most popular target for magic potions may be the person who carries around a few extra pounds. Time was, fat was good. An ad for Grove's Tasteless Chill Tonic (one and a half million bottles sold in 1879) boasted: "Makes children and adults as fat as pigs." But that time is long gone. Among the more unusual weight-loss schemes we've heard about:

- A bandage weight-loss wrap. Supposed to let you lose inches while cleansing environmental poisons from your body, this dandy won a 1999 Slim Chance Award for most outrageous gadget from the editor of *Healthy Weight Journal.*
- *The Svelt Patch.* It contained something called concentrated fucus, which claimed to melt fat even while you slept and even if you ate up to five times daily. The price for twenty weeks of patches was $132.
- *SlimAmerica's four-drug formula.* It was supposed to slim while you ate up to six times a day. "Yes, this amazing new super-formula will overwhelm fat like Cary Grant overwhelmed your grandmother!"
- *Amazing Seaweed Weight Loss Soap.* Its lather "penetrates the skin to break up fat Globules as you wash." "Unwanted pounds and inches literally scrub right off."
- *The Fat-Be-Gone ring.* It bears a passing resemblance to a gold-colored paper clip twisted into a coil and takes its cue from what it calls a Japanese belief: that a person can lose weight in various parts of the body by applying pressure to one or more fingers.
- *Fat Trapper and Exercise in a Bottle.* "Never, ever, ever, ever have to diet again," said an infomercial that featured former baseball player Steve Garvey along with an array of beautiful but voracious people gobbling pizza and fried chicken.

Many people believe that claims for health products must be true or they wouldn't be allowed. Not so. Sure, the government has some authority over such matters. The FDA has jurisdiction over labeling of drugs—defined as any product intended for use in the cure, mitigation, treatment, or prevention of a disease. If a product is sold with a drug claim that lacks FDA approval, the agency can issue a warning letter. If it has proof of problems, it can remove a hazardous (or worthless) drug from the market. The FTC has authority over advertising and marketing of over-the-counter drugs and can challenge unsubstantiated advertising, investigate questionable trade practices, and seek injunctions and civil penalties for violations.

Moreover, some marketers do get their just deserts. In early 2000, the FTC announced that Enforma Natural Products of Los Angeles, maker of Fat Trapper and Exercise in a Bottle, had agreed to stop making deceptive claims and to pay $10 million to the people who bought its products or to the U.S. Treasury if refunds to buyers were not practical. Enforma's chief executive said the company would "stand by our excellent products" and was settling the case to avoid a costly legal battle.

Often, however, as soon as one questionable offer is quashed, another pops up. Two factors are likely to make life harder for government watchdogs. The first is the boom in nutritional supplements. In 2000, according to Information Resources, Inc., Americans spent nearly $600 million on herbal supplements alone, bought at food stores, drug stores, and mass-market retailers. Although manufacturers of supplements cannot make express or implied claims about treatment or prevention of disease without prior FDA review, they can escape that review if they claim only that their product affects the body's "structure or function." "Prevents heart disease" would not be allowed without prior approval, yet "maintains a healthy circulatory system" would be allowed. The FDA bears the burden of showing that a supplement is unsafe or mislabeled before it can restrict or ban its use.

The second factor likely to make policing of health products harder is the Internet. A recent survey by the Pew Internet and American Life Project showed that some fifty-two million Americans seeks health information on-line at least once a month. Clearly, not all that information is beneficial: The FTC and public health advocates from twenty-five countries identified eight hundred fraudulent web sites during only two days of searching the internet, one day in 1997 and one in 1998.

The bottom line is that you have to look out for yourself. When it comes to health claims, be wary of these phrases and marketing techniques:

- A product is labeled a quick and effective cure-all for a wide range of ailments.
- A promoter uses words like "scientific breakthrough," "miraculous cure," "exclusive product," "secret ingredient," or "ancient remedy."
- A product is advertised as available from only one source, with payment required in advance.
- A promoter promises a no-risk, money-back guarantee. Many fly-by-night operators aren't around long enough to comply.
- A product promises a quick fix.

- An ad includes paranoid accusations, as in: Drug companies are in cahoots with doctors to suppress the product and keep you from securing proper treatment.

Perhaps hardest to assess are two other favored techniques, the use of "medicalese," often attached to the name of a doctor and/or research institution, and the use of testimonials by "real" people who got dramatic results.

Who are those people in lab coats posing before bookcases or peeking from behind beakers? Long ago, they were memorialized by *Ballyhoo* magazine, a compendium of mock ads, in the person of Harvey K. Poop the Second—the man (the magazine said) "who first proved statistically that four out of five have pyorrhea and that nine out of ten believe it." ("Pyorrhea" was an advertising euphemism for gum disease, now referred to as "gingivitis.")

Sometimes the people in lab coats are actual doctors who have been quoted without their knowledge. In 1985, we reported on Colon Cleanse, which claimed to remove "all the bad bacterias from the body which may be brewing many kinds of sickness." The ad bolstered its claims by citing a Harvard Medical School faculty member, a chief of the Gastrointestinal Clinic at the Mount Sinai Medical Center in New York, and an associate professor of medicine at George Washington University. When we called those doctors, they told us they'd never heard of Colon Cleanse. And when we called the distributor of the product, its president told us that he saw the doctors' names in an article on constipation in the *National Enquirer*.

As for the regular Joes and Jills who testify, often convincingly, about the charms of these potions, the FTC says their claims must reflect their honest experience or opinion. If their experience could be atypical, the ad is supposed to say so. If the ad says a celebrity uses the product, that must be true. Testimonials can make quite spectacular claims. Some of our favorites:

The *New York Tribune* of 1841 told of Jane Demee, who had tried to rid herself of a disease that was eating away her face. "I am satisfied," she wrote, "that my life has been preserved and my health entirely restored by the blessing of God and the use of Bristol's Fluid Extract of Sarsaparilla."

In 1929, a quack named Matthew Richartz quoted one J. C. Meyers of Charleston, South Carolina, in a promotion for Eksip, essentially magnesium carbonate, talc, and starch. "I am a living advertisement for Eksip," Meyers was supposed to have said, "for if it had not been for Eksip and God's blessing, I would have been in my grave today." Alas, in 1929, Meyers *was* in his grave. He had died five years before of diabetes, the disease that Eksip supposedly cured.

In 1996, *Consumer Reports* received a flyer for Bilberry, described as a natural approach to improved eyesight. One testimonial, from a Sister Paula Matthew: "This stuff is great! Now would a nun lie to you?"

The point is, it's hard to know. > > >

Are they conserving paper?

Shown here—actual size—is a small portion of the information slip enclosed with Naprosyn. That's an anti-inflammatory medication for ailments such as arthritis, gout, and bursitis. But why are we telling you that? It says so right there on the slip, clear as day. Much of the slip is devoted to contraindications, warnings, and precautions, so be sure to read every word.

—October 1991

NAPROSYN®
(naproxen)

National PharmPak Services, Inc.
Zanesville, OH 43701

55154-3802
55154-3803   **8/90**
55154-3804

The rabbit died

A California reader sent us a coupon advertising a book from Family Research Institute called *Preconception Sex Choice* ($4.95 plus postage and handling). The ad copy says, somewhat ambiguously, that "Our research has shown that the odds are really close to 95-5 that in a given time in the female's life cycle the child will be of one sex or the other." (Not to pick nits, but we would have put the odds at close to 100 to zero.)

Still more amusing was the book's thirty-day money-back guarantee. Most people would need more like nine months.

—September 1992

Please send me a copy of
"Preconception Sex Choice"

One hump or two?

Curious about these important words, we called matchbook-maker D. D. Bean, where a worker reassured us. The notice is "a bit of advertising humor." Nothing dire will happen if you use the matches to light a Marlboro—or a birthday candle.

—January 1994

DO NOT DISTRIBUTE THESE MATCHES
OR TOBACCO PRODUCTS TO MINORS

CAMEL
LIGHTS

LOW TAR
CAMEL TASTE

CLOSE COVER BEFORE ST

IMPORTANT:
These are CAMEL matches.
They have been specially
designed to light CAMEL
cigarettes. And only
CAMEL cigarettes.

Smoke and mirrors

Here, a brochure for a program that uses herbs and a scented liquid to break a nicotine addiction. Never having tried the program, we'll reserve judgment as to whether "27 all-natural herbal ingredients" can make anyone stop smoking. What intrigues us is a boast in the brochure: Quikquitz "has a tremendous success rate among those who have used the program and remained off tobacco products." In other words, for any people the program worked for, the program worked.

—July 1996

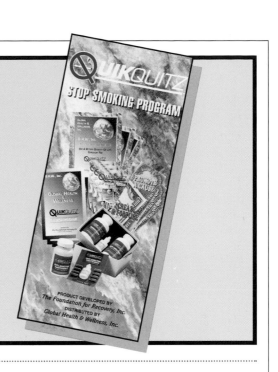

Wha??

We wanted to say something about this product, too—but our teeth fell out.

—March 1999

Press 4 for weird

"This is, well, unbelievable," the e-mail message said, and it listed a toll-free number. Curious, we called. Here's what a man's voice said:

"Hello, you've reached the Brown & Williamson Tobacco Corporation. If you're an adult smoker, 21 or older, welcome. If you're not 21 and not a smoker, please hang up now. Before any information is exchanged, there will be age verification, so again, if you're not 21, please hang up now.

"Good. Now that it's just us, there's something that we, Brown & Williamson Tobacco, would like to tell you. It may be a little soon, but, well, it just feels right. [Enter shmaltzy piano music.]

"We, the Brown & Williamson Tobacco Corporation, are in love—with you. Yup, you heard right. Brown & Williamson Tobacco is in love! We're a giant corporation, and you make us feel like a little kitten. Thank you, lover. By

the way, the other tobacco companies hate you and think you're ugly. They told us so. Now, press 1 to be put on our mailing list."

We pressed 3, to talk to a customer-service representative, and a recorded message told us we'd be connected to "the real people at Brown & Williamson who can assist you."

So, we asked the woman who got on the line, is this really Brown & Williamson? Yes, she said, and her answer was confirmed when we checked the toll-free number with a representative at corporate headquarters. "The one about the guy who loves you?" she asked. "It's legit."

Oh—when we pressed 2, to ask another rep for a nearby store that sells Lucky Strike unfiltered cigarettes, how did she verify our age? She used that time-honored, foolproof method: She asked for a date of birth.

—*December 1999*

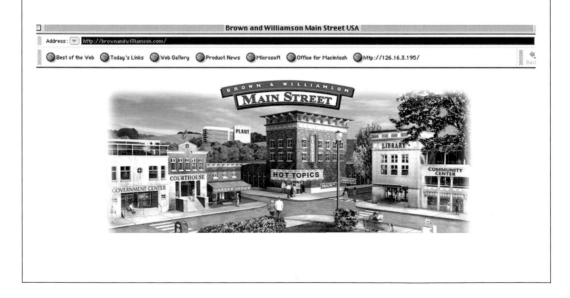

Odd offer of the month

We know what they mean, but still . . . (The free book comes with a subscription to the *American Journal on Addictions*.)

—*August 1997*

Time for a new crystal ball

This letter was signed by Joyce Jillson, who is . . . well, it's hard to tell. Her title is "Director Professional Assessments, Associate for Psychic Involvement," and the letter is littered with such important-sounding return addresses as "Record Office for Detailed Documents," "Files/ Psychic Developments and Results," and (our favorite) "Office of Direct Contact with Known Individual." Joyce offers to provide the letter's recipient, a fellow named Forest, with information about "An Important Matter [ref: 1019ff]" that may affect his life. "I and my associates have such great experience in these matters, and as professional psychics we have proven ourselves to be accurate in such things." Too bad Joyce wasn't there for Forest ten years ago— when he died.

—*May 1998*

RESULTS AND DEVELOPMENTS
CE OF DIRECT CONTACT WITH KNOWN INDIVIDUAL

JOYCE JILLSON
DIRECTOR PROFESSIONAL ASSESSMENTS
ASSOCIATE FOR PSYCHIC INVOLVEMENT

ADVISORY FROM RECORDS OFFICE

PREPARED DOCUMENTS TO RECEIVER
PERSONAL ASSESSMENTS

INFORMATION CONTACT WITH IDENTIFIED RECEIVER

COMPLETION PAPERS

RECORD OFFICE FOR DETAILED DOCUMENTS

MAIN INFORMATION CENTER   ASSESSMENTS AND DETAILED VERIFICATIONS   CONVEYANCE INTERPRETATIONS   INDIVIDUAL RECORDS

THE MATTER OF:

Forest

The Matter Of:
•••••••••••••••••• 3-DIGIT 275
Forest
NC 27549-9803

Identification Completed

--8/97--Records Office
Contact Required
Article No: [ref:1019ff]

ARRANGEMENTS ENACTMENT
The office of: Joyce Jillson
TO: Forest

IDENTIFICATION MADE   September 25, 19

Dear Forest,

We'll try tea leaves

Recently, two psychics had great predictions for Ron, a reader from Stanford, California. Helen Archer, a Psychic Planetologist from East Hanover, New Jersey, wrote to say she had a vision about him. "You had won a very large cash prize (something like $211,721.06 or even more)," she noted. Failing to explain what something like $211,721.06 might be, she added that Ron was on the verge of entering a limited-duration "triple-high-jackpot cycle" during which he could expect to turn his life around. Good thing, too, because she knew through an unnamed contact that Ron had "had a lot of tough breaks—even though you really deserve to have money. . . ."

Helen claimed she could help Ron find the lotto numbers that would net him that cash prize. To get the numbers, Ron was to send Helen a request and a check. Helen crossed out her usual fee of $150. "For you," she scribbled, "only $20 is necessary."

We wonder whether Helen is acquainted with Professor H. P. Wellington, a fellow New Jerseyan and the President of Future Forecasters. "Ron," H. P. exclaimed in a letter, "suppose I told you that there is at least $9770.00 in cash waiting for you!

"You see Ron, last Tuesday 7 of our researchers were conducting a controversial experiment (Project X711) in psychic phenomena. . . . While each was sitting in their own private cubicle, they were instructed to write down the name of the individual they had focused on. . . . The end result was amazing! The name that was written down was your name. . . . Even more incredible, [they] reported having seen the number 9770 over and over again beside a stack of cash while in a trance-like state of mind!"

Ron could find out how, when, and where to collect his money for FREE, H. P. said, but the processing fee was, you guessed it, $20.

When we called the Better Business Bureau, we found out that "Helen" and "H. P." are indeed acquainted: Their addresses are used by Fight Back International Corporation, which also operates as The Lottery Doctor and Pot O'Gold.

All this leaves one question unanswered: If the psychics are so good, why didn't they know Ron would spurn their pitch and send their letters to us?

—*March 1994*

No lions, no tigers, no bears

Spectrum's Chewable Multiple Vitamins say they're "for kids" and have cute, colorful animal shapes on the front. No wonder the buyer thought there would be cute, colorful animal-shaped vitamins inside. Nope. No cuteness, no color, no animals. Just these plain, gray-brown, round tablets. Wonder what Spectrum has in store for adults.

—*September 1999*

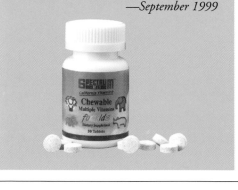

Eyewash indeed

The ingredients of Bausch & Lomb's Sensitive Eyes Saline Solution are below left; the ingredients of its Eye Wash, below right. Similar, no? The price wasn't, though, for a New York reader. She paid nearly twice as much for four ounces of Eye Wash as for an equal amount of Saline Solution. True, Eye Wash comes with a little cup, but that would hardly seem worth $2.10.

We asked a consumer-affairs represen-tative at Bausch & Lomb about the dis-crepancy. "The formulas are different in percentages," she told us, though that's not evident from the package. Still, why should one cost so much more? Because, she said, the packaging is somewhat different and the two products are not approved for the same use—Eye Wash can go in your eye, Saline Solution can't. Oh.

—November 1998

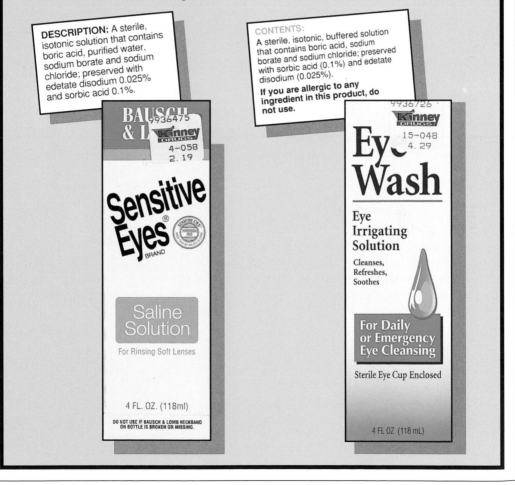

DESCRIPTION: A sterile, isotonic solution that contains boric acid, purified water, sodium borate and sodium chloride; preserved with edetate disodium 0.025% and sorbic acid 0.1%.

CONTENTS:
A sterile, isotonic, buffered solution that contains boric acid, sodium borate and sodium chloride; preserved with sorbic acid (0.1%) and edetate disodium (0.025%).

If you are allergic to any ingredient in this product, do not use.

BAUSCH & L
9936475
Kinney DRUGS
4-058
2.19

Sensitive Eyes®
BRAND

Saline Solution

For Rinsing Soft Lenses

4 FL. OZ. (118ml)

DO NOT USE IF BAUSCH & LOMB NECKBAND ON BOTTLE IS BROKEN OR MISSING.

9936726
Kinney DRUGS
15-048
4.29

Eye Wash

Eye Irrigating Solution

Cleanses, Refreshes, Soothes

For Daily or Emergency Eye Cleansing

Sterile Eye Cup Enclosed

4 FL OZ (118 mL)

An ad a day keeps the doctor away?

As a New Jersey reader perused the *Journal of Longevity* (subtitle: *Medical Research Reviews in Preventive Medicine Fields*), he began to notice something cozy about the placement of advertising. After an article about arthritis came an ad for MSM, a substance dubbed "the key to restoring joint mobility & comfort." After an article about hair problems came an ad for NHC, a "nutritional hair complex." On it went through sex life, aging, breathing difficulties, high blood pressure, weight loss, water retention, memory loss, gum infections, and eye problems. At the end of the magazine was a form revealing that all the touted nostrums could be ordered from the same company, Gero Vita International of Ontario, Canada. Curious about the journal's ties to Gero Vita, we checked the web address listed under the masthead (www.gvi.com), then called the phone number posted there, only to find that the journal is actually published by—surprise!—Gero Vita.

—*July 1999*

I *think* I can, I *think* I can

For $125 plus shipping and handling, Athena II guarantees "fuller, firmer breasts" within sixty days—with an increase in bustline, the ad says, of up to 3½ inches. Is it minor surgery? An implant? A cream? Nope. Here's a hint: It involves audiocassettes and a workbook. Give up? Athena II builds the bustline by using "advanced visualization, guided imagery and meditation to unleash the power of your mind/body connection" and "substantially increase bloodflow to your breasts." Our medical consultant's comment: "Think your way to a C cup? Ludicrous."

—*June 1999*

"I USED ATHENA II, AND MY BREASTS GREW 2 INCHES! ATHENA II WORKS!"

Gulp!

Two readers bought Osteo Bi-Flex, a nutritional supplement, because the pills were called "easy to swallow." When the readers opened the bottle, they found pills longer and far fatter than the one pictured on the label (package and pill are shown actual size).

—*May 1999*

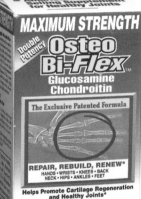

Sundown's Maximum Strength Osteo-Bi-Flex PATENTED FORMULA of Glucosamine and Chondroitin is manufactured and laboratory tested under strict quality assurance programs and meets the requirements for safety, quality, purity, identity and strength.

EASY TO SWALLOW – ACTUAL SIZE
See other side panels for more information.

Fancy pants

Slimmer shorts, the ad says, are made of neoprene and "generate heat to melt away unwanted fat and hydric deposits." Hydric deposits? That's moisture to us. Translation: The shorts make you sweat.

—May 1999

That's *Dr.* Editor to you

The editor of "Selling It" is now a Registered Therapeutic Specialist. Did this involve years of study? Hardly, but we've gotten ahead of ourselves. Some time ago, the International Association of Therapeutic Specialists, of Grand Rapids, Michigan, asked a New York doctor to join its ranks. Instead of being pleased, he was peeved, and sent us the invitation. The mission of the association, it said, is "to enhance each member's knowledge, skills and overall *earning potential*" (emphasis courtesy of the doctor). It continued: "You will be setting yourself apart from the competition by elevating your professional status to its highest level and reassuring your clients, while enjoying the prestige of having our impressive membership certificate on your office wall." Cost for the first year's membership: $65.

Curious, our editor recently asked for her own application, and while she wasn't sent the letter excerpted above, she did receive two applications. One asked for no payment for the first year and $50 per year thereafter; the other asked for $65 up front. She filled out the freebie honestly, claiming bachelor's and master's degrees (in English and journalism, as it happens) and asking to be qualified in weight loss

and insomnia. Although the application required no proof of abilities in the specialties suggested—whether catastrophic illness, stuttering, or regression therapy—she figured a successful diet twenty years ago and advice to her sleep-deprived husband might suffice if she were queried further. However, no explanations were needed. She received this certificate, which will hang in her office, where she'll do her best to advise impressed clients. Here's a start: Exercise does help in losing weight, and warm milk puts at least one insomniac to sleep.

—January 1999

Take two tubs and call me in the morning

For years, pharmaceutical companies have paid representatives to pitch their wares to doctors, but here's a new approach that makes you a company representative. To get a pound of Smart Balance Spread free, you're directed to take a package to your doctor, who must sign a form stating, "I have received Smart Balance Margarine Spread from my patient and agree to try it," and add his or her address and phone number. Then you're to send the form, plus proof of purchase, to Heart Beat Foods. You may get a free tub of spread, but here's what a North Carolina reader wants to know: Who pays for the doctor visit?

—December 1998

Herb blurbs

This catalog for the *Herb Companion* magazine is full of praise from readers: the woman who salvaged a baby shower by curing her daughter's heartburn with an herbal remedy from the magazine; the New Yorker who indulged a passion for growing herbs by stacking them as instructed by the magazine; the reader who credits an article "jam-packed with herbal beauty recipes!" with giving her gift ideas. The testimonials are quite detailed, but if you squint at the bottom of one page, you'll see something else—they're "dramatized." What does that mean? Although they represent the type of things people have said, a spokeswoman for the Herb Companion told us, they're basically made up.

—August 1998

Love potion strikes out

"There I was in Kroger's supermarket last Tuesday," says Mary James, the smiling brunette, "when along comes this man behind me. He is about 5'5", overweight by at least 30 pounds and not very good looking. . . . But the strangest thing happened." What? A romantic, um, dalliance. After all, the man was wearing Le' Natural cologne. Among the tamer promises to men who splash it on: "3 out of 4 sexy women will go crazy over you. . . guaranteed!"

What's in Le' Natural? "Five very potent sexual molecules (called 'Pheomones') that excite the neurons."

(We think they mean pheromones, but this is no time to quibble.) Our sensory panelists describe the odor as "sweet floral with slight woody undertone; reminiscent of baby powder."

Being a testing magazine, of course we had to try this stuff. We paid $24.95 for one ounce and asked four men to apply it (we covered its name), wait 5 minutes (it "works in 4-5 minutes!"), then tell us about any unusual reactions from women during the rest of the day (it "works up to 9 and one-half hours!").

Phil went to a Grand Union, where he saw many women. Not one found him "very tempting"; in fact, no one noticed him. Eric went to a concert, where no women "lit up like a firecracker with passionate, red-hot desire!" Dave had a bit more success—his girlfriend said, "Mmm. You smell good"—but he doesn't usually wear cologne. And women on the subway offered only glazed-over silence. Jim was our star: At a business lunch, a female acquaintance elevated their relationship from handshake to hug-and-kiss. But even Jim was not "flooded with scores of wanting women!" which was reassuring to his wife.

Then again, we should have known the claims were iffy. Le' Natural, operating out of Brooklyn, New York, has an unsatisfactory rating with the Better Business Bureau. When asked for the names of ten satisfied customers, states the bureau report, the firm would oblige only if the bureau "made it worth their while."

—*November 1998*

The more you visit, the more you need

After announcing the introduction of its Computer Eye Drops, designed to relieve eyes that have become tired, stressed, and strained by staring at a computer, Bausch & Lomb invites the reader to, you guessed it, visit the company's web site.

—*June 1998*

An ounce of prevention

Maybe we wouldn't be so bothered if Eli Lilly and Company hadn't underlined "completely," colored it yellow, and printed the explanation below the ad in tiny type: "*Degree of prevention can vary from person to person." Looks as if *Axid AR* can prevent heartburn completely except when it can't.

—*December 1996*

Heartburn wars

Doctors have "endorsed" Tagamet more often than Pepcid—237 million prescriptions to 36 million, this ad says. That's a 6.6-to-1 ratio, as the bar graph shows. But wait. Let's trace the asterisk in that graph to the bottom of the page. There, tiny type reveals that the figures cover Tagamet prescriptions written since 1977 and Pepcid prescriptions written since 1986. During the years when doctors had a choice between the two drugs, the ratio is more modest—about 3:1. It's enough to give a statistician heartburn.

—*July 1996*

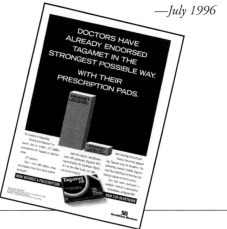

A paper infomercial?

A New Jersey reader found this question-and-answer "guide to choosing the right OTC pain reliever" in her pharmacy and began to browse through it. When she noticed that most of the answers praised acetaminophen, she checked the back of the pamphlet. Sure enough, this "service to patients" came from McNeil Consumer Products Company, maker of—you guessed it—Tylenol brand acetaminophen.

—October 1995

Are-U-Serious?

H ow about spraying your way to weight loss? Spray-U-Thin is an appetite suppressant, the ad says, with an active ingredient that has been "proven safe and effective." That ingredient is phenylpropanolamine. It's used in diet pills, diet gum, and nasal decongestants, but delivery by mouth spray is a new one on us. And it's a new one on the U.S. Food and Drug Administration, which considers Spray-U-Thin a new, unapproved drug and says the manufacturer's claims of appetite suppression are currently illegal.

Oh—the manufacturer points out that Spray-U-Thin also freshens breath.

—February 1994

Looks great.
I said, LOOKS GREAT!

A California reader sent us an offer from Magnatone Quality Hearing Instruments, maker of the Magnatone Rechargeable hearing aid. "To acquaint the public with the latest strides in the hearing industry," the offer read, "Magnatone is giving a free, actual size, non-operating replica for you to try in the privacy of your home." It was the word "non-operating" that stopped our reader. Admittedly, appearance can play a role when it comes time to buy a hearing aid. But, our reader pointed out, "I thought people might be primarily interested in how much it helped their hearing."

—December 1993

Aware of the benefits of exercise but being somewhat lazy, we were intrigued by the ad a reader sent for Jogging in a Jug. Could it be that sipping this "tart-tasting tonic" of vinegar and fruit juice would keep us from having to run a mile or two? We asked Third Option Laboratories of Tuscumbia, Alabama, for a free brochure right away.

Back came an explanation of how the product works: "Vinegar is like a natural solvent for the body, cleaning crystal deposits that are the base of clogged arteries and arthritis." And back came glowing testimonials: "I use to get up in the morning still tired, but now . . . I'm ready to start my day." And "My husband's cholesterol has dropped from 217 to 190 . . . and he can close his hands from arthritis after three months."

But while giving with the right hand, the literature takes away with the left, stating that the concoction's creator, Jack McWilliams, "is careful to note that the Food and Drug Administration will not allow him to make any health claims about his drink."

When we checked for ourselves on the benefits of vinegar, reality hit. CU's medical consultants "know of no health benefits from vinegar ingestion." Our nutritional experts were "at a loss to explain these claims." They suggested we check medical journals (and told us, helpfully, that vinegar was good for cleaning certain surfaces).

A search of medical journals as far afield as Ethiopia and Australia revealed that vinegar (or acetic acid) is an essential first-aid treatment for the sting of the box jellyfish, can kill bacteria on parsley if the parsley is dipped in it, and can reduce the size of an ossified mass if injected and followed by ultrasound. It can also cause a loss of tooth surface if ingested frequently.

It's time to confess that we ordered Jogging in a Jug. It's sold in stores for $5.95 per 64-ounce bottle, though you could concoct your own vinegar-and-juice mix for about $3.25. We ordered a lot of Jogging in a Jug, since it's shipped only by the case. Total cost: $46.09.

When we left a bottle out for staffers, they sipped rather than guzzled. That could be because, according to our sensory experts, the drink leaves a distinctly sour taste in the mouth. Last we looked, the jug was down a few ounces, but no one was sprinting down the hall for seconds.

—*February 1994*

Politically incorrect

"A woman is different than a man," says the television commercial for Correctol laxative, and no one can quibble with the concept. As for the rest of the ad, however, there's plenty to criticize. Although Correctol bills itself as "the gentle laxative made especially for women," it's nearly identical to the laxative Feen-a-mint. Both are made by Schering-Plough, and they have the same active ingredients in the same amounts.

Well, there are a few differences. Correctol is a pink pill in a pink box, whereas Feen-a-mint is a white pill wrapped in blue. Correctol has a special price, usually about 15 percent higher at wholesale than Feen-a-mint's. (A spokesman for Schering-Plough cited extra costs for advertising and distribution.) And the boxes of Feen-a-mint we bought warn pregnant or nursing women to seek the advice of a health professional before using the product. The U.S. Food and Drug Administration says that such a warning is not necessary; still, it's interesting that Schering-Plough chose to leave a similar note off boxes of Correctol, the woman's laxative.

—*December 1993*

Healthy request

After ordering a free trial copy of *Health* magazine, a Wisconsin reader received a "Friendly Reminder" from the publication requesting payment for a subscription. "The enclosed invoice needs your immediate attention," read the note. "The price of your subscription may seem like a small amount to you, but it means a lot to us." In fact, it meant a lot to our reader, as well. The bill requested $1,265.85 for 352 issues—more than twenty-nine years' worth of *Health*. Even if he took all the health advice to heart, our reader, now seventy years old, suspected that the subscription would exceed his needs. Was it an innovative sales technique? More likely a computer glitch, said the supervisor of *Health*'s subscription office, adding, "I don't think it would be a very effective marketing ploy."

—*September 1993*

New!
Half the strength!

A Connecticut reader alerted us to this NEW! IMPROVED bottle of Triaminic Syrup, a children's cold medicine. The new bottle looks similar to the old one, although it comes encased in a cardboard box. And it costs the same—about $8 for eight ounces. But our reader noticed a big difference: The amount of active ingredients has been cut in half, and the dosage, accordingly, has risen from one teaspoon to two. She wondered if this wasn't the same as doubling the price. We asked Sandoz Pharmaceuticals Corporation, Triaminic's maker, to clear things up.

A Sandoz spokesman emphasized the positive. "We've improved the flavor," he told us, "and changed the dosing regimen." (Meaning you take twice as much.) Furthermore, he pointed out,

Old label

EACH TEASPOONFUL (5ML) CONTAINS, phenylpropanolamine hydrochloride 12.5 mg and chlorpheniramine maleate 2 mg. OTHER IN-

EACH TEASPOONFUL (5ML) CONTAINS: phenylpropanolamine hydrochloride, USP 6.25 mg and chlorpheniramine maleate, USP 1 mg.

New label

"We didn't raise the price when we brought out the new product line."

Thank goodness for small favors. But we'd be happier if the price had been cut along with the active ingredients.

—*November 1992*

1 for you, 99 for me

S everal readers have sent us an appeal from the "National Cancer Research Center," identified as "A Project of Walker Cancer Research Institute." The letter asks the recipient to gather donations from neighbors and send the money to the NCRC. A dense block of text on the back of the letter provides enlightening information on this charity—if you can decipher it. Here's the gist: Of the $2,422,477 raised by the NCRC last year, less than one penny of every dollar went to cancer research. The rest paid a professional fund-raiser,

defrayed fund-raising costs, administered the fund, settled lawsuits arising from previous misleading solicitations, and paid for "public education."

An example of that education: the recommendation here, printed on the letter. Hardly the sort of information the public can't find anywhere else.

—*June 1992*

C -
H - SIX CANCER CHECKS
E - Check up - get one each year
C - Healthy Air - STOP smoking
K - Eat foods that help fight cancer risk
S - Check your home for cancer causing hazards like radon
  - Keep your workplace free of cancer hazards
  - Sun in moderation - and always use a sun block.

A bald ruse

Many people whose hairline is in retreat have heard of Rogaine, Upjohn Company's brand of the prescription drug minoxidil. Originally developed as a blood-pressure medication, minoxidil seems to stimulate modest hair growth for as long as it's used. Now Upjohn has introduced Progaine Shampoo, "scientifically formulated to clean thinning hair."

One would be forgiven for assuming that Rogaine and Progaine had something in common. There's the similar name and package design; the fact that Upjohn makes both; and, not least, a relatively high price—we paid $4.30 for five fluid ounces, which makes Progaine one of the most expensive shampoos on the market.

Wondering if there were indeed similarities, we translated Progaine's ingredients label, which includes such tongue twisters as methylisothiazolinone and cocamidopropyl betaine. Translation: Progaine contains mild detergents, conditioners, a foam booster, a moisturizer, and assorted other ingredients found in many other shampoos. But that's all. It has no minoxidil and no special power to slow the loss of hair.

—October 1992

Vitamins vs. radiation

If you frequent health-food stores, you may have seen the "Anti-Radiation, Anti-Jet Lag Kit for Air Travelers." It contains a packet of Emer'gen-C, a vitamin C powder you mix with water, and Super-Gram III, a multivitamin tablet. In a blurb full of gee-whiz claims and celebrity names, manufacturer Alacer Corporation of Irvine, California, calls those nostrums "the two most powerful food supplements in the world."

Alacer's radiation-protection claim hinges on a laboratory finding that vitamin C can neutralize free radicals—unstable, highly reactive forms of molecules that can attack the body's cells. But performance in a test tube is a far cry from performance in a body, whether at sea level or at thirty-five thousand feet. It's an even greater leap to assume that the packets would actually help ward off whatever cancer risk is posed by radiation during flight.

In any case, the risk to high-fliers is extremely small. A round-trip flight between Chicago and New York exposes you to about one-fifth the radiation of a chest X ray.

—*August 1991*

The green pill for Sneezy, the yellow pill for Dopey

Drixoral Plus tablets, a product of Schering-Plough HealthCare products, are green. They bill themselves as a remedy for many ailments, including nasal and sinus congestion, runny nose, sneezing, itchy and watery eyes, fever, and minor aches and pains. Schering's newer tablets, Drixoral Sinus, are yellow. They're marketed for sinus sufferers rather than for more generalized misery. The lists of ingredients reveal that the two products are one and the same. But Drixoral Sinus tablets sell for over a dollar more than Drixoral Plus.

Our phone call to Schering's customer relations department confirmed that the new product is new in name and color only. "It's really just a marketing strategy," the Schering representative confided.

—*January 1991*

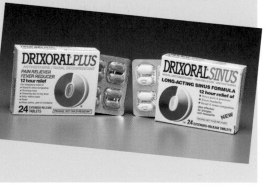

WHAT A DEAL

"Surely it is asking too much to expect the advertiser to describe the shortcomings of his product? One must be forgiven for putting one's best foot forward."

David Ogilvy,
Confessions of an Advertising Man

Some offers take the word chutzpah—impudence, gall, brazen nerve, incredible cheek, and unmitigated audacity—to a new level.

In the late 1800s, people who sent money for what was advertised as a "Potato Bug Eradicator" received two wooden slivers with the instructions, "Place the potato bug between the two sticks of wood and press them together." A "steel engraving, approved by the U.S. government" turned out to be a postage stamp. And an "additional benefit" cited years ago by a United of Omaha insurance policy? The company would refund any premiums paid beyond the month of the insured person's death.

The asterisk and barely readable type are the premier icons of such flimflammery. They're often partners in deception with the word "free" and an assortment of brightly colored statements such as "Improved!" that stand out on packages and are known in the business as, of all things, "violators." According to the FTC and the Better Business Bureau, asterisks should not be used to change substantially the meaning of any advertising statement. That guideline is often ignored, but even we at *Consumer Reports* were surprised in 1986, when an appliance dealer in New York listed a built-in oven for $289.88, with an asterisk revealing that oven doors were extra. (The dealer told us the door clause gave the customer more choice.) A

Window Maid product we spied in 1988 was "Guaranteed! You'll never wash windows again.*" Never believe "never." What the words meant, the asterisk explained, was never again *this year*.

The FTC also says advertisers can't use fine print to clear up misimpressions. If an ad says, "Lose 10 pounds in one week without dieting," for example, fine print can't say, "Diet and exercise required." Is anyone paying attention? Hardly. They haven't been for years. In the mid-1900s, railroad owner Elliott Springs papered the South with maps that showed his tracks crisscrossing fifteen states. Below was the headline "The Lancaster & Chester Railway System." Lower still were the small words "and connecting lines." Springs's railroad was a mere twenty-nine miles long. In 1981, a magazine carried an ad offering celebrity addresses. For $2, you got twenty-seven hundred names. Just names. The addresses, a small footnote revealed, cost 50 cents each—for a total of $1,350, if you bought every one. A newspaper advertised a condo in Atlantic City for $89,900. "Impossible?" it asked. Well, yes. In smaller type was the revelation that you'd pay that price only if you recruited "two friends, relatives, or business associates" to fork over the same amount and buy the condo *with* you. A newspaper ad for a "FULLY LOADED VINTAGE WINE CELLAR" revealed elsewhere that "We've loaded it with extras [like a deluxe handle], you add the wine."

"Free" should also set off warning bells. The FTC says a free product must be legitimately free, and that all terms, conditions, and obligations must be stated clearly and conspicuously. Yet we receive countless ads for free products that blatantly state a price nearby. And the cost of freedom can be high. "Free waterbed," said a 1986 ad for a Pennsylvania company. Just one catch: You had to buy a fill-and-drain kit (a $3 value) for $159. In 1985, a Ramada Hotel advertised a "free hotel room" but imposed a parking fee of $55 per night—and parking was mandatory.

Obviously, an offer of a "free" extra on an established product isn't supposed to involve a price hike. Nevertheless, *Consumer Reports* readers—who take comparison-shopping to new heights—have provided us with plenty of examples in which it does. Back in 1979, a reader bought nearly identical packs of razor blades on the same day at the same store. One held five blades for $1.29. The other promised one free blade but sold for $1.49. Another reader noticed an offer for "Shetland Sweaters with FREE monogram, $18–$20. (Take $2 off the price of sweater if purchased without monogram.)"

Moreover, a company is not supposed to keep a "free" offer going for a long time. Yet for some fifteen years, Mary Carter Paints advised consumers that they could "buy a can and get the second can free." The FTC charged that the ads were deceptive because the only price offered, in the absence of any other prices, was really the price for two cans.

Sometimes it takes more than a quick check to discover what's bad about a deal. Consider the tale of the kid who offered customers at his lemonade stand all the lemonade they could drink. When a patron asked for more, he said, "That's all you can drink."

How would you know that the statement "Famous nationally advertised 35 mm camera with accessories only $10—unbelievable but true!" was actually unbelievable and false unless you bought the thing, as *Consumer Reports* did? We received a cheap model of a brand we'd never encountered, without the claimed exposure meter or parallax correction. Its "newest spaceage materials" were plastic.

It took a phone call for a reader to determine that the price a Minnesota company listed for its shoes was not per pair but per shoe. And it took a little thinking to realize that maybe Lancôme's offer of a free seven-day supply of Primordiale Nuit skin cream left consumers a little short. Why? Elsewhere in the offer, the company promised visibly younger skin tone and texture after *eight* nights.

What other rules apply to price? The FTC says a seller can't:

- Sell an item regularly for $7.50, then sell it for $10 for a few days, then offer a "bargain" of $7.50.
- Say "reduced to $9.99" when the former price was $10.
- Say "Retail Value $15, My Price $7.50" when only a few remote stores in the area charge $15 and almost all nearby stores charge about $7.50. (In any case, suggested retail prices are often a fiction. Says the Better Business Bureau, "Today, only in the rare case are all sales of an article at the manufacturer's suggested retail or list price.")

When fixed prices first appeared on products, they were seen as an advance over the old way of doing business—bargaining. The Quakers thought fixed prices helped purge possessions of their emotional power, and people who were poor bargainers could feel they were treated equitably. But what factors drive fixed prices unreasonably high?

Sometimes, the fault lies at least partly in ourselves. Some of us want to own the most expensive thing out there—Jean Patou, Inc., proudly pitched Joy perfume as the "costliest perfume in the world." Some of us won't believe that "inexpensive" and "high-quality" can live in the same neighborhood. Years ago, an ad agency determined that the price of 69 cents that a company had set for its product Car-Nu was too low. The average auto owner, the agency told the company, was afraid a product that cheap would damage the car's finish. The agency's recommendation: Add an innocuous new ingredient, enlarge the can a bit and sell it for $1.69. The strategy worked, *Advertising Age* pointed out.

We may be attracted by a product's surroundings. Bath soap nestled in a cute setting in a little boutique will get a far different reaction than the same product stuck on a metal shelf in a warehouse chain. Long ago, *Women's Wear Daily* reported that a store sold a particular blouse in three different departments and in three different ways. At one counter, the blouse cost $3.95. In another location, the blouse was packed in a stock box and cost $4.95. In a third location, a similar blouse (with better buttons and an embroidered pocket) was packed in a special box and cost $9.50. Each blouse sold successfully to its particular clientele.

Some of us can't resist an image or a hot brand name. Back in the 1970s, a "Selling It" column quoted *Forbes* magazine, which discussed the marketing of Jack Daniel's whiskey by owner Brown-Forman. "With heavy advertising and promotion," the magazine said, "Brown-Forman creates a premium image for its products, then charges a premium price for them, thus both recapturing the extra advertising costs and making higher profits as well. For example, you can buy bourbon whiskeys for around $6.50 a bottle in New York, but Brown-Forman's Jack Daniel's can set you back $8.10. Does it cost over $1 extra to make Jack Daniel's? That's a foolish question."

Even cuisines have an image that can be reflected in their price. Have you ever wondered how a French restaurant gets away with charging $30 for a soupçon of coq au vin while a Chinese restaurant charges $8 for a platter of chicken that could be finished off only by a pair of fullbacks? We wondered, too. So we asked Ruth Reichl, the editor-in-chief of *Gourmet* and former restaurant critic for the *New York Times*. In part, the reason for higher French-restaurant prices is slower turnover of tables and higher rent paid for fancy venues. But there's another factor. "For whatever reason," Reichl said, "Americans will not pay a lot of money for Chinese food. They have it in their heads that it's supposed to be cheap."

Finally, some people succumb to a questionable deal because it makes them feel special. The Glo-Worm Society, a private club founded by "funloving young ladies," promised a *Consumer Reports* employee benefits beyond his wildest fantasies. "We have something that you want, and you have something that we need." Our employee forked over $30 for an executive, um, membership. He received: a questionnaire, a pitch to subscribe to a newsletter, a pitch to send funds or other names to the society, advice on making himself more appealing, an "intimate gift" purporting to be a diary excerpt, and—ta-da—a membership pin.

Our favorite questionable offers in the flattery category come from companies that manage to find talent even when it's deeply buried. And our favorite story comes from Pierre Berton, who in his book *The Big Sell* told of responding to three ads that solicited poems or song lyrics for appraisal. There was no charge up front, and Berton submitted an intentionally bad poem under the name of his nine-year-old daughter, Penny. Although Berton had hoped to disqualify Penny by rhyming the words "friendship" and "endship," all the firms thought her quite gifted. His next move was to attach his seven-year-old daughter's name to a poem called "Wantcha." It consisted of that word repeated twelve times, followed by "all the time." Then came the word "Needta" repeated twelve times and followed by "make you mine." Well, as you may have guessed, that one was accepted, too. All Berton had to do to achieve fame and fortune was fill out a contract—and send money. > > >

Die now, pay less

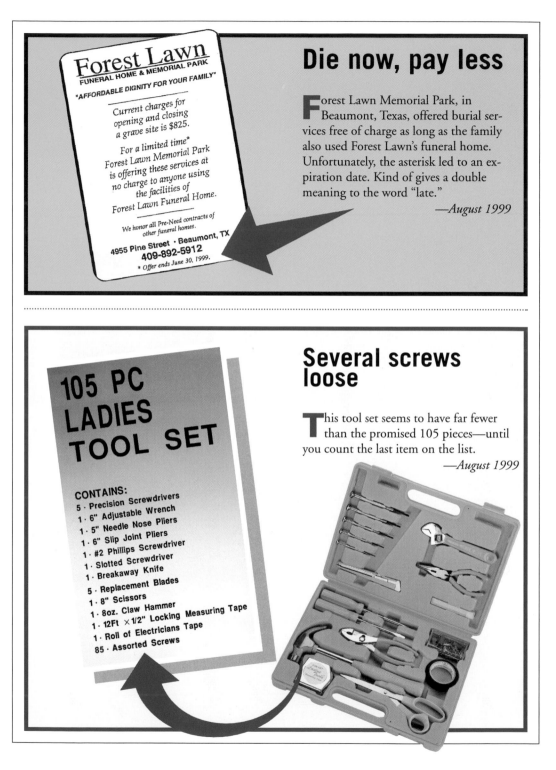

Forest Lawn Memorial Park, in Beaumont, Texas, offered burial services free of charge as long as the family also used Forest Lawn's funeral home. Unfortunately, the asterisk led to an expiration date. Kind of gives a double meaning to the word "late."

—*August 1999*

Forest Lawn
FUNERAL HOME & MEMORIAL PARK

"AFFORDABLE DIGNITY FOR YOUR FAMILY"

Current charges for opening and closing a grave site is $825.

For a limited time* Forest Lawn Memorial Park is offering these services at no charge to anyone using the facilities of Forest Lawn Funeral Home.

We honor all Pre-Need contracts of other funeral homes.

4955 Pine Street · Beaumont, TX
409-892-5912
* Offer ends June 30, 1999.

Several screws loose

This tool set seems to have far fewer than the promised 105 pieces—until you count the last item on the list.

—*August 1999*

105 PC LADIES TOOL SET

CONTAINS:
5 · Precision Screwdrivers
1 · 6" Adjustable Wrench
1 · 5" Needle Nose Pliers
1 · 6" Slip Joint Pliers
1 · #2 Phillips Screwdriver
1 · Slotted Screwdriver
1 · Breakaway Knife
5 · Replacement Blades
1 · 8" Scissors
1 · 8oz. Claw Hammer
1 · 12Ft × 1/2" Locking Measuring Tape
1 · Roll of Electricians Tape
85 · Assorted Screws

More than five easy pieces

We've seen 12-piece cookware sets that count lids and handles as pieces, but this ad from the Sharper Image catalog was a new one on us. The picture reveals, and the order clerk told us, that the 311 pieces on this Tool Wall include all the little clips and hooks from which the tools hang. No wonder the wall's average cost is "less than 97 cents per item."

—August 1994

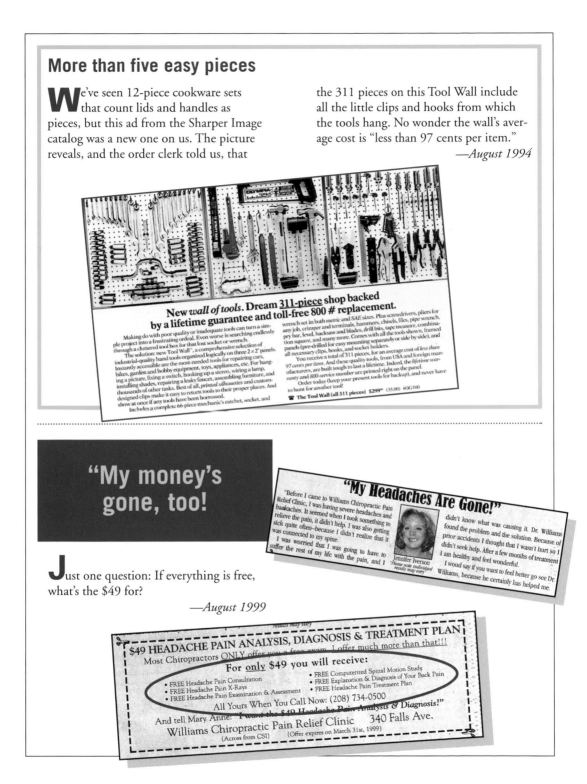

New wall of tools. Dream 311-piece shop backed by a lifetime guarantee and toll-free 800 # replacement.

Making do with poor quality or inadequate tools can turn a simple project into a frustrating ordeal. Even worse is searching endlessly through a cluttered tool box for that lost socket or wrench.

The solution: new Tool Wall™, a comprehensive selection of industrial-quality hand tools organized logically on three 2 × 2' panels. Instantly accessible are the most-needed tools for repairing cars, bikes, garden and hobby equipment, toys, appliances, etc. For hanging a picture, fixing a switch, hooking up a stereo, wiring a lamp, installing shades, repairing a leaky faucet, assembling furniture, and thousands of other tasks. Best of all, *printed silhouettes* and custom-designed clips make it easy to return tools to their proper places. And show at once if any tools have been borrowed.

Includes a complete 66-piece mechanic's ratchet, socket, and wrench set in both *metric* and *SAE* sizes. Plus screwdrivers, pliers for any job, crimper and terminals, hammers, chisels, files, pipe wrench, pry bar, level, hacksaw and blades, drill bits, tape measure, combination square, and many more. Comes with all the tools shown, framed panels (pre-drilled for easy mounting separately or side by side), and all necessary clips, hooks, and socket holders.

You receive a total of 311 pieces, for an average cost of *less than 97 cents per item*. And these quality tools, from USA and foreign manufacturers, are built tough to last a lifetime. Indeed, the *lifetime warranty and 800-service number* are printed right on the panel.

Order today (keep your present tools for backup), and never have to hunt for another tool!

The Tool Wall (all 311 pieces) $299⁰⁰ (35.90) #OG100

"My money's gone, too!"

Just one question: If everything is free, what's the $49 for?

—August 1999

"My Headaches Are Gone!"

"Before I came to Williams Chiropractic Pain Relief Clinic, I was having severe headaches and backaches. It seemed when I took something to relieve the pain, it didn't help. I was also getting sick quite often—because I didn't realize that it was connected to my spine.

I was worried that I was going to have to suffer the rest of my life with the pain, and I didn't know what was causing it. Dr. Williams found the problem and the solution. Because of prior accidents I thought that I wasn't hurt so I didn't seek help. After a few months of treatment I am healthy and feel wonderful.

I woud say if you want to feel better go see Dr. Williams, because he certainly has helped me.

Jennifer Iverson
Please note individual results may vary

$49 HEADACHE PAIN ANALYSIS, DIAGNOSIS & TREATMENT PLAN

Most Chiropractors ONLY offer you a free exam. I offer much more than that!!!

For only $49 you will receive:

- FREE Headache Pain Consultation
- FREE Headache Pain X-Rays
- FREE Headache Pain Examination & Assessment
- FREE Computerized Spinal Motion Study
- FREE Explanation & Diagnosis of Your Back Pain
- FREE Headache Pain Treatment Plan

All Yours When You Call Now: (208) 734-0500

And tell Mary Anne: "I want the $49 Headache Pain Analysis & Diagnosis!"

Williams Chiropractic Pain Relief Clinic   340 Falls Ave.
(Across from CSI)   (Offer expires on March 31st, 1999)

You're a poet, but you don't know it

"New Poetry Contests," the ad announced, and two of our editors—let's call them Jack and Jill—were intrigued. Would the National Library of Poetry include their work in one of its "forthcoming hardbound anthologies"? Might they even be among the "talented poets" awarded prizes? The editors submitted their worst efforts. Jack sent the pretentious "Days' End," below right. Jill, a skeptical type, sent "Ode on a Rose," which (using the first word of each line) spells out this hidden message: "Is this for real, Let's find out now, O perhaps it's true, But we doubt it." What did the return mail bring? Praise—and a recognition that the poets' egos, and their wallets, could be outsized.

The first missive cited the poets' "unique talent," said their poems had reached the contest's semifinals, and expressed a wish to publish the poems. Jack's would be in The Fabric of Life, Jill's in Winds of Freedom.

This mailing and others sent to Jack (who was more diligent about responding) offered: an author's biography, to be published with the poem (cost to the poet: $20); a copy of the anthology, at a "special discount" ($49.95 plus $7 postage); a copy of the poem on a plaque ($38); an audiotape of the poem ($29.95 plus $4 postage); an invitation to join The International Society of Poets (dues $95 or $125, in different mailings, plus $12 shipping and handling); laminated cards printed with the poem (24 for $19.95 plus $4 postage and handling); another chance to order anthologies and plaques; and an invitation to submit another poem. Total cost: at least $279.85.

Jack awaits the arrival of the anthology he ordered and any winnings. Meanwhile, he'll content himself with a freebie the library sent: an "Editor's Choice Award" certificate offering "congratulations on your creative achievement." Move over, Maya Angelou.

DAYS' END

Where once the savage current roared
the barren bed turns hard and dry
its aspect bitter, pinched and crazed
Where once days past and days to come
mingled in wild, unruly league
a point, a geometric nil, remains
And shades in mournful prospect launch
the verity that numbs the core:
The promised resurrection will not be

—June 1998

We think that we shall never see/the end of this

Our resident poet, who caught the eye of the International Society of Poets with his brooding "Days' End," has received the anthology containing that poem. But that's not all. The society said it wanted to award him an "International Poet of Merit" medallion and asked him to compete for the title Poet of the Year—all at a three-day symposium in Washington, D.C. Cost: $595, plus hotel. The National Library of Poetry, at the same address, would like to publish a new effort by our poet (he can buy the book for $49.95). And Premier Melodies, a third outfit at the same address, wants to set his poem to original music—rock, soul, country, gospel, folk, or other ($299, which includes five "free" cassettes).

Roses are red, violets are blue, success is sweet, but he's not sending any more money.

—October 1998

THE NATIONAL LIBRARY OF
POETRY

Sentimental [and short] journey

For its U.R. the Star videos, Sentimental Journeys Inc. uses a customer's photo as the face of the star of one of several cartoons, thus "personalizing" the video by turning a child (or adult, or pet) into Hercules or Circus Star, for instance. The brochure promises "a 13 to 15 minute adventure. Similar to a Saturday morning cartoon without the commercial interruptions." When a reader complained about a video she had bought, we ordered our own, *Amazing Kid,* and submitted the photo of a four-year-old we know. As our reader had found, our kid's adventure was abbreviated: It lasted all of eight and a half minutes, at a cost of almost $3 per minute. True, no commercials interrupted the cartoon. Instead, one big commercial—how the videos are made and how to order more —came at the end. It lasted three minutes—time for Amazing Kid to have saved at least one more planet from destruction.

—September 1998

MAKING THE TAPES

The start of something big

For answering thirteen questions about travel ("When you are on vacation, do you enjoy sightseeing?" and so on), a reader learned that he'd earn a FREE GIFT! from American Express. The gift was attractive—a Smithsonian guide called *The Pacific: Alaska and Hawaii*—and the reader was about to fill in answers when he noticed he'd be receiving something else "in further appreciation of your participation." Namely, more guides—guides to the Great Lakes, the Southeast, Appalachia; to the Far West, the Northern Rockies, the Heartland. In all, fifteen more guides, one every six weeks. But these wouldn't be free. He could take the trouble to send the books back, but if he kept them, he'd be charged, automatically, the "Questionnaire Participant" price of $19.95 per book, plus $3.95 postage. Total outlay: $358.50, or $27.58 per question.

—August 1998

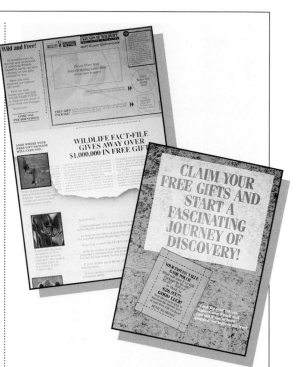

The snowball effect

Want to be a Friend of Wildlife? Just send in the gift claim certificate, and you'll get a preview set of twelve cards providing information about an animal or environmental topic, along with a package of additional information. If you keep the cards, you pay $4.95. Then, every three weeks, you'll get a new packet of twelve cards for $5.45 plus postage and handling.

You can cancel at any time, but if you don't, how long does this go on? In all the material sent (only part of it is shown here), just one tiny line tells you. The complete set is 1,188 cards, sent over about five years. The total cost: about $530, plus postage and handling. That would buy a lot of nature books.

—February 1996

Singing the blues

From Time-Life Music comes this offer of a free CD or cassette—*Blues Legends*. But though you'll "send no money" and face no "risk" or "obligation" at first, the small print reveals that the CD or cassette is free for only ten days. If you keep the music, you'll need to pay $9.99 plus shipping and handling. Then, you'll automatically receive more blues CDs or tapes that cost even more— $16.99 or $14.99, plus shipping and handling.

—March 1998

Oh, and by the way . . .

The offer below left and the "P.S.," shown underneath, appear in a Renaissance Cruises brochure sent to a California reader who had cruised with Renaissance before. When he called to receive his binoculars, he was told to read page 3. There, without a photo or color tint to make it stand out, is the message: "And, as a special 'Thank You' to our Past Guest, when you personally call 1-800-251-8098 *and book your Seychelles Islands, African Safari and Ancient Egypt Cruise Tour,* you will receive 2 COMPLIMENTARY PAIRS of Focus-Free Compact Binoculars" (italics ours). Cost of cruise plus binoculars? $4,500 to $8,000. Our reader passed.

—February 1998

See the "P.S." inside for a special Past Guest "Thank You" Offer from Renaissance Cruises and The Sharper Image®!

copyright © The Sharper Image

Frank Del Rio
Executive Vice President

P.S. As a special "Thank You" to our Past Guests, if you personally call our Past Guest Special Services Desk at 1-800-251-8098, you will receive 2 Complimentary Focus-Free Compact Binoculars – a $300 value – from The Sharper Image® and Renaissance Cruises.

Keep on surfin'

With these utility programs, the packaging says, you get 120 hours of Internet access free. And the asterisk? The inset magnifies the fine print. Better brew a lot of coffee. You have to use up all 120 hours within five days after you've signed up.

—April 1998

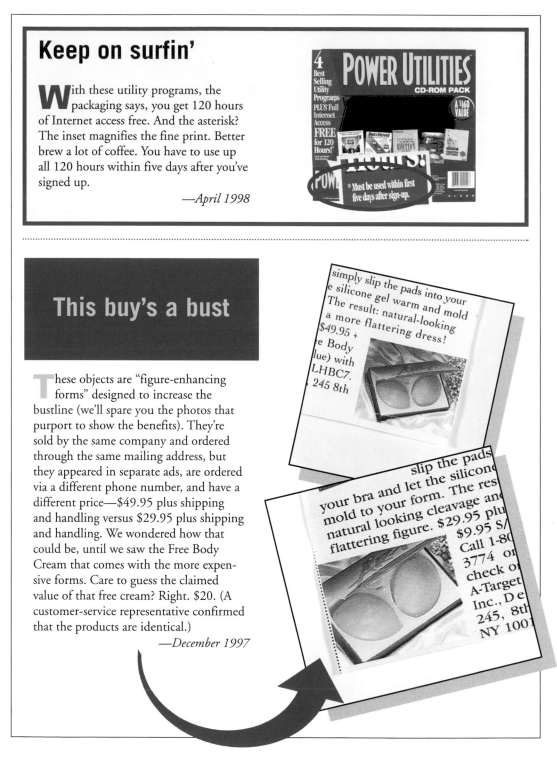

4 Best Selling Utility Programs PLUS Full Internet Access **FREE** for 120 Hours!

POWER UTILITIES
CD-ROM PACK

A $160 VALUE

* Must be used within first five days after sign-up.

This buy's a bust

These objects are "figure-enhancing forms" designed to increase the bustline (we'll spare you the photos that purport to show the benefits). They're sold by the same company and ordered through the same mailing address, but they appeared in separate ads, are ordered via a different phone number, and have a different price—$49.95 plus shipping and handling versus $29.95 plus shipping and handling. We wondered how that could be, until we saw the Free Body Cream that comes with the more expensive forms. Care to guess the claimed value of that free cream? Right. $20. (A customer-service representative confirmed that the products are identical.)

—December 1997

simply slip the pads into your e silicone gel warm and mold The result: natural-looking a more flattering dress! $49.95 + e Body lue) with LHBC7. 245 8th

slip the pads your bra and let the silicone mold to your form. The res natural looking cleavage an flattering figure. $29.95 plu $9.95 S/ Call 1-8(3774 or check o A-Target Inc., D e 245, 8th NY 100

No, not that Columbia

How about earning credit for a college degree by eating in exotic restaurants, playing golf, or taking photographs? How about earning that degree in twenty-seven days? How about paying $1,695 and up? That's the deal at Columbia State University in Metairie, Louisiana.

To apply, you send information about your professional background and a check for $35. Upon acceptance, you can wear a school ring ("always impressive" to potential employers, a brochure says). For a bachelor's degree, you read at least one textbook, then take an open-book test or summarize the book. That's it. For a master's, you also write a six-page "thesis"; for a Ph.D., a twelve-page "dissertation." The school examines your work and an "experiential portfolio" you've filled out (that's where your golf comes in), then sends your diploma and transcripts—which, the brochure says, "of course do not indicate that [the degree] came from a non-traditional school, even though it's a U.S. Government approved school, as opposed to an out-dated, archaically traditional, school whose main purpose is greed."

We called the school to ask what organization accredits Columbia State. The Council on Post-Secondary Accreditation, replied our admissions counselor, a Mr. Roberts. That group claims to be "the only legitimate school-accrediting association in the world." It's not. In fact, a spokesman at the U.S. Department of Education told us, no government-recognized accrediting group has approved Columbia State. An attorney with the department said it doesn't regulate schools that receive no federal financial aid (and Columbia State is among them). We also called Louisiana's board of regents, which said the school is exempt from the board's oversight because it's exempt from taxes. The board sent us to the state attorney general's consumer office, which has received a few complaints about the school but can only mediate between school and complainants. The moral: Student beware.

Oh, and another thing. Don't plan on attending reunions. Columbia State's "administrative office" is a Mailboxes Etc. in a strip mall. And that building on the booklet? A reader informed us that it's the Lyndhurst estate in Tarrytown, N.Y., a mansion once owned by railroad baron Jay Gould. The booklet's printer, said Mr. Roberts, "went overboard."

—*November 1997*

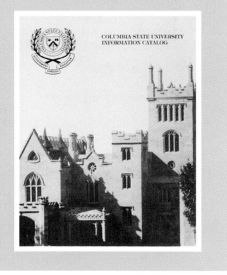

Eskimo snow job

Could be, but then again . . .
—February 1997

Could be a
better value
than shoes
costing up to
$89.93

We'll wait for Exxon's offer

A Florida reader received these mailings from Shell and Citgo. Included was the same letter (aside from the change in company name), the same order form, and illustrations of what appear to be the same three products for sale—a pocket appointment book, a "deluxe" appointment book, and a calendar. What really intrigued our reader was each company's assessment of the products' value. "Three great products for 1996," Shell boasted, "worth $58.15 yours for just $3 each!" And the identical three great products from Citgo? "Worth $42.85 yours for just $2 each!"

—June 1996

Calling all climatologists

Rain or shine? Everything? Free? There had to be a catch in this ad for Suffern Fine Furniture, in New York. And there it was, in fine print at the bottom. "If it rains 1 inch or more OR is over 95°F according to the Official National Weather Station in Central Park, N.Y.C. on SEPT. 7, 1996 between the hours of 9 am and 5 pm, everything you purchase between Aug. 22 and Aug. 26 will be absolutely free (excluding tax and delivery)."

—January 1997

Up a creek

Just imagine the sales pitch if Gazelle sold cars instead of canoes: FREE AUTOMOBILE (*Requires the purchase of four tires for $20,000).

—October 1995

Seek and ye may find

Obviously there's a catch in this ad from Redlands Roofing (only a doghouse roof could be covered for $250), but a California reader said we'd have to look hard to spot it. He was right. It took us nearly a minute to notice the pale-peach OFF that lies beneath the type.

—November 1995

The price of freedom

The way we figure it, AirTran, the company that made this offer, will charge you $50 to "take a child to Orlando for free!" And another $50 to take the child back home.

—May 1995

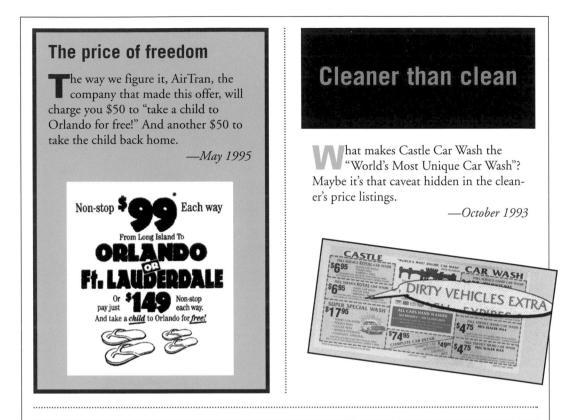

Cleaner than clean

What makes Castle Car Wash the "World's Most Unique Car Wash"? Maybe it's that caveat hidden in the cleaner's price listings.

—October 1993

What we wouldn't do for a buck

Last spring, we came across a refund certificate worthy of note. All you had to do to receive a dollar was buy one bag of Kingsford Charcoal, one package of Adolph's Marinade in Minutes, one can of Pam cooking spray, one package of Tyson Holly Farms chicken, and one package of either Dixie Livingware plates or cups or Northern napkins. Clip the UPC symbols from all the products. Throw them in an envelope with the refund certificate, a piece of paper with your name and address, and receipts from the purchases (with prices circled and product names written beside each). Buy all products between May 23 and June 13, and have the envelope postmarked by June 13. And, of course, affix a stamp to the envelope. Nearby coupons gave discounts for the products involved, but we figure that by then, anyone but Scrooge was too weary to clip them.

—August 1993

Why are these men smiling?

Here, poster boys from our favorite get-rich-quick ads of 1994. The man on the left is smiling because he has filled out a lot of blank pages. For that, he has earned $3,000 per page. Apparently, a cache of these mysterious Million Dollar Pages were discovered in the garage of a dead man who had become rich by filling them out. "Now," says DTV Systems, "it's your turn!"

DTV doesn't say what you write on pages or why you write it. It does say the procedure involves an "amazing secret process" and that your writing will go faster with a free high-performance pen "specifically designed for filling out pages such as these." Cost for the first hundred pages: $19.95.

The man in the middle is smiling because he has mailed a lot of letters. If he has been as lucky as N.L. of West Palm Beach, Florida, he's made $126,000 by stuffing two thousand printed, stamped envelopes for various U.S. firms. For $19, Harvey Wilson sends a manual that reveals how to mail letters for profit.

The man on the right is smiling because he has typed a lot of numbers. These are "not just any numbers," says DTC Publishing, "but secret numbers that can bring YOU tens of thousands of dollars." They brought Ann B. of Beverly Hills, California, $150,000 in one year. Who wants the numbers? Financial institutions, which are "anxious to get this because their profit depends on it." For—yup—$19.95, DTC will tell you how to get the numbers.

The Better Business Bureau has no detailed record on these companies, but it gave us a general warning about work-at-home scams: "Very seldom if ever do you make back your initial investment."

—*March 1995*

Free for a fee

If our mail is any indication, the cost of "free" is on the rise across the land. A Tennessee pizzeria serves up one large pie for $5.55. Its "fast free" delivery service will bring the same pie to your door for $6.93. The New York Palace Hotel offers a weekend rate of $175 per room, per night. Twenty dollars more will buy "free parking!"

Then there's Green Giant's puppet. "The adorable Sprout Hand Puppet can be yours FREE when you buy the vegetable products listed on the left," reads the newspaper ad. All you have to do is mail in proofs of purchase from "20

Frozen and 40 Canned or Jar" vegetable products. If your pantry isn't large enough to stock that much food, you can get a free Sprout for just three proofs of purchase and $5.95.

—*May 1993*

Zero-karat gold

The good news arrived in a bright yellow envelope postmarked Dallas. "You have been pre-approved for a gold card with a $10,000.00 line of credit," Credicorp Inc. informed readers in Illinois, Indiana, Nevada, and Virginia. "Mail your $29.95 annual fee . . . to activate your credit immediately."

But don't expect a Visa or Mastercard.

In fact, don't expect a major credit card at all. According to the Dallas Better Business Bureau, Credicorp's "gold card" can be used only to make purchases from that company's catalog—a fact never mentioned in the mailing. The bureau has received more than four hundred complaints from consumers who felt duped by the offer. Some recipients actually used the card but never received the merchandise they ordered.

Last year, authorities in Texas and Arkansas filed suit against Credicorp Inc. (a.k.a. Credit Card Center and Fafco), alleging that the company's mailings violate the states' laws on deceptive trade practices. Credicorp recently agreed to give refunds to Arkansas residents. The Texas suit is pending. Meanwhile, Credicorp Inc. continues digging for gold. Yours.

—*May 1993*

A new wrinkle

A New York reader spotted these two jackets six pages apart in a recent J. Crew catalog. What, she wondered, was the difference between the $88 "well-worn barn jacket" (prewashed, lined in cotton madras, with a water-resistant cotton canvas shell, corduroy collar, and turnback cuffs) and the $98 "broken-in barn jacket" (identically endowed)? "Ten dollars," answered the J. Crew sales clerk we reached through the catalog's 800 number. "It's basically the same thing with a more worn-in appearance," she explained. Why the higher price? She didn't know.

We hung up, phoned J. Crew's toll-free number again, and posed the same question to another sales representative. "The broken-in barn jacket is more expensive," we were told, "because it's very popular now."

—*February 1993*

"broken-in"

"well-worn"

Sub-standard

One day not long ago, a Boston reader picked up his mail and found two subscription promotions from *Time* magazine. One offered a year's subscription to *Time* plus a "free" clock for $31.20. Each said the offer was "the guaranteed lowest introductory rate."

Besides the obvious conclusion that the free clock costs about $10, we wondered what "guaranteed lowest rate" means. We asked a Time executive to explain. He admitted that having different prices called "guaranteed lowest" is not, perhaps, "a high ground of consumer marketing." To us it seems that "guaranteed lowest" means "lowest unless you discover otherwise."

—*October 1992*

TIME

ACT NOW

All professionals responding to this notice before the date indicated will receive TIME at over $120.00 off the Cover Price. This offer is the guaranteed lowest introductory rate and is not available to the general public.

To receive one year of TIME for just 60¢ an issue—a 79% savings off the cover price and the guaranteed lowest rate available anywhere—mail this receipt in the enclosed envelope.

ACT NOW

All professionals responding to this notice before the date indicated will receive TIME at over $110.00 off the Cover Price. This offer is the guaranteed lowest introductory rate and is not available to the general public.

To receive your FREE GIFT and get one year of TIME for just 79¢ an issue—a 73% savings off the cover price—mail this receipt in the enclosed envelope.

Mathcads

Recently, within two days, the mathematics department of Southern Connecticut State University received three pieces of mail from MathSoft, a company in Cambridge, Massachusetts. "For just $99 (a savings of $396 off the list price!)" MathSoft offered Mathcad 3.1, "an award-winning, versatile software tool for teaching math and science." Another MathSoft letter in the same batch of mail peddled the software for "just $79." The next day brought MathSoft mailing number three: "just $49." When it wrote us, the math department was holding out for a few days in the hope that a $9 offer would arrive.

MathSoft's marketing director told us the company regularly tests different prices, "but this wasn't as good a test as we would have wished." It seems the company's mailing house inadvertently omitted the top line of each address—the names of the specific faculty members meant to receive the various offers.

We wondered, had the mailing gone glitch-free, would the professors not have put two and two together and discovered the discrepant "bargains" offered to their colleagues? "We've learned that sending different offers to one school is not a good idea," conceded the MathSoft marketer. "Educators tend to talk to each other."

—January 1993

A shady deal

Many readers have sent us a magazine ad for free sunglasses available by mail from a company called Solex Quality Optics. The ad raves about "high fashion, high quality, [and] UV protection," among other things. It pictures many styles of sunglasses, grouped into price categories labeled "compare at" $160, $90, and $56 per pair. Best of all, up to four pairs are "yours free" as part of a "market test." All you have to do is pay "postage, handling, and insurance."

We sent for one pair from each category. The shipping charges were a little steep: $19.95 for the costliest "free" pair, $9.95 for the middling pair, and $6.95 for the cheapest: $36.85 in all. When the glasses arrived a few days later, we noticed that Solex had lavished a total of $2.71 on postage.

The glasses didn't look very expensive. They looked like cheap sunglasses. Which is what they are. They have polycarbonate plastic lenses, which are tougher than glass though more easily scratched. None were even polarized. As for the UV protection claim, that's nothing special. When we looked at sunglasses a few years ago, all the ones we tested did a good job of blocking ultraviolet light.

The Admiral, top right, a "compare at $56 pair," has an inherently weak hinge design we would strive to avoid. Below the Admiral is the Quasar, a $90 type. It has an uneven coating of the material used to reduce glare.

There's nothing wrong with wearing cheap sunglasses. Last time we tested sunglasses, we found that some pairs costing $5 to $15 afford just as much sun protection as the costly types. But at least when you go into a discount store to buy a pair, you're not conned into believing, even for a minute, that they're worth more than the few dollars you're paying.

—March 1992

Not a good "Bi" for homeowners

The last word in creative financing seems to last only until the next word. Sometimes it's best not to listen. That's the case with BiSaver, a Virginia company and the author of a letter, full of boldface type and exclamation points, that invites mortgage holders to repay their home mortgage in biweekly installments. After paying BiSaver a startup fee of $365, a homeowner gives the company half a month's mortgage payment every two weeks. Once a month, BiSaver forwards a month's payment to your bank. Since twenty-six half-payments equal thirteen monthly payments, you effectively make one extra monthly payment per year. BiSaver sends that payment to your bank in two installments six months apart.

While the sales letter emphasizes the savings that come from speeding up mortgage repayment—the process really can cut years off the term and thousands of dollars off the interest charges—the letter neatly sidesteps the fact that no one needs this service. Just about any mortgage holder can prepay a lender directly. At one's own convenience, rather than BiSaver's, one can arrange to make an extra monthly payment each year (marked "for principal only") and save as much.

—February 1992

RE: Mortgage Loan No.:   819384-9
    BiSaver ID No.:   8869-013-131-4

Dear Customer:

IF YOU'D LIKE TO: SAVE $51,934.34 IN SCHEDULED PAYMENTS; AND,
                  KNOCK 8 YEARS AND 4 MONTHS OFF YOUR MORTGAGE . . .
                  CALL 1-800-368-8800. IMMEDIATELY!

For a limited time, you can slash both the time and expense that stand between you and mortgage-free homeownership . . . with amazing ease.

HOW? Through the "BISAVER" BIWEEKLY MORTGAGE COST REDUCTION SYSTEM.

WITH BISAVER, YOU'LL PAY AN AMOUNT EQUAL TO HALF OF YOUR REGULAR MONTHLY MORTGAGE PAYMENT ON A BIWEEKLY BASIS (EVERY 2 WEEKS). THIS WILL CUT $51,934.34 AND 8 YEARS AND 4 MONTHS OFF YOUR MORTGAGE!

HOW CAN BISAVER BE SO SIMPLE AND SAVE ME SO MUCH TIME AND MONEY? Since there are 26 biweekly periods in a year, each year you will have made the equivalent of one extra mortgage payment to reduce your debt—painlessly. Every extra cent goes to reduce your principal, powerfully attacking the total cost of your mortgage. What's more, you'll build real equity faster and be able to pocket considerably more cash if you sell.

IS IT EASY? Yes. You won't even have to write out mortgage checks. BiSaver is automatic! Simply designate the checking account from which you'd like BiSaver biweekly transfers to be made.

We've set up a special automated system that handles it all for you. It makes the biweekly transfers from your account electronically and credits your mortgage on its regular monthly due date—like clockwork.

HOW MUCH WILL IT COST? There is a one-time Start-up Charge of $365. This nonrefundable charge may be paid by check, MasterCard or VISA.

BiSaver works wonders on your present loan (no need to refinance). So forget the major expense and hassle some people find with refinancing.

Your part is simple.

More like fool's gold?

The Shell Oil company offered holders of its credit card the chance to buy a diminutive replica of the old U.S. $20 gold piece—in "Pure 24K, 100% Solid Gold!"—for $19.90 plus $1.95 for postage and handling. Touting the merits of 24-karat gold, the graph pictured here purports to show gold content at various karats. (Note how it makes 41.67 percent gold look like 15 percent in the far-right bar.)

Although an actual-size photo reveals that the coin has the approximate diameter of a thumbtack, it took a call to the company to determine the coin's weight:

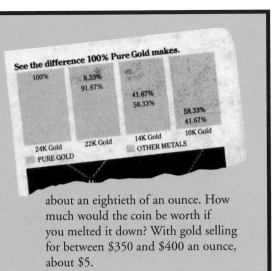

about an eightieth of an ounce. How much would the coin be worth if you melted it down? With gold selling for between $350 and $400 an ounce, about $5.

—September 1991

Mickey Mouse offer

A magazine ad placed by American Express and Walt Disney World led two readers, and us, into Confusionland. The promotion, called Kids Go Free, is for adults who take children to a Disney resort and charge a four-night deluxe package on an American Express card. So far, no questions. But the ad also says that adults traveling without children get $300 off. Hmmm. If it costs $300 more to show up with a kid, how do Kids Go Free?

We obtained price quotes from several Disney reservations people and received several explanations for the mystery. A typical Kids Go Free package, we were told, costs $2,266 for two adults and two children. Without two kids? $1,666, or $300 less per child.

One agent opined, "It's double occupancy. The kids share your room."

Another: "That [price] is what the computer tells us. It doesn't say why." A third explained that what we were seeing wasn't an extra charge for children, but an extra discount for no children. The last one sort of makes sense.

We think the best bet for parents who want to visit Disney World by themselves is to ask for the Kids Go Free program. Then tell the clerk the kids are staying at home.

Welcome to Never-Never Land.

—September 1991

Maybe the half-full size

Note this ad for *Herbal Creme de Mint Natural Toothpaste*. Doesn't the big headline seem to promise a big tube? The tube in the ad, reclining atop the box, is quite visibly a seven-ounce size. The contents of the pump dispenser to its right weigh in at 4½ ounces. But the order form mentions only a three-ounce tube, available "for for $1 in postage and handling" (another touch we always appreciate).

When we called the company, we were told that there was no mistake. Three ounces was the full size, because it's "one of the sizes we normally sell." What about the even fuller seven-ounce tube in the ad? "It looked better next to the pump."

—August 1991

Just say yes

Most credit-card holders are familiar with the confirmation letter that follows on the heels of a new credit card—the letter that says to call if you haven't received the card and to do nothing if you have. Now a company called Hot-Line Credit Card Service has found a way to turn that confirmation notice into a sales contract.

Shortly after one of our staffers received a new Mobil credit card, he got a notice bearing the Mobil logo and asking if he'd received his card. If not, he was to call an 800 number. If so, he was urged to sign at the X and return the notice by a specified date.

Anyone giving the document a quick look might miss the paragraph stating that the signature automatically enrolls the signer for lost-card insurance, at $12 a year.

—June 1991

How about a loan shark?

With the prime interest rate at this writing between 9 and 10 percent and consumer credit available for 12 to 20 percent, how do you get people to borrow money at almost 24 percent per year? Beneficial Massachusetts Inc., a finance company, thinks it has the answer: Dangle a big check in front of them and hope they cash it. If they do, they're hooked.

A Massachusetts reader recently received from Beneficial an unsolicited check for just over $1,500. There was nothing deceptive in the offer: A disclosure statement spelled out the terms quite clearly, right down to the 23.7 percent annual interest rate and the $614.18 cost of the loan over thirty-six months.

It would take some comparison shopping, however, to show you that the check in hand represented the most expensive legal loan in the state of Massachusetts. Practically any other personal loan would be a better deal, whether it came from a bank, a credit union, or even a credit card.

—June 1991

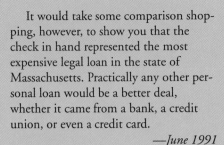

Something fishy

Perhaps Fisher Boy fish sticks illustrated more of a parable than it meant when it pictured this fishing lure trailing three quarters. The accompanying coupon is worth only 55 cents.

—March 1991

Gem-of-the-month club

Holsted Jewelers of Hicksville, New York, sent a "Gift Certificate" to a Texas reader. It offers a "free" ring that costs $2 plus $3.99 shipping and handling. Accepting the Royal Austrian Faux Blue Topaz Ring commits the customer to receive automatic bimonthly shipments of other costume jewelry, sight unseen, at $39.99 each. Plus shipping, naturally. The junk jewelry may be new, but selling merchandise through a negative-option plan has a familiar—and unpleasant—ring.

—February 1991

"Free" and "limited" redefined

A flyer received in early July by a Delaware reader promised "great news": a two-year membership in the Wilmington Swim Club, a health club in New Castle. According to the flyer, the membership is "valued at over $800.00 and it is yours FREE!" In fact, the word "free" appears three times. The flyer warns that the offer is limited: "[You] must call or stop by . . . within the next 48 hours."

An additional little detail is relegated to the last paragraph: Each member must pay a "maintenance fee" of $99 a year to "maintain a clean and professional facility." That same paragraph also confesses that the $99 annual fee entitles you to only a few basic facilities. In case you're harboring any hopes of actually swimming at this "swim club," or in case you want to use the sauna, tanning facility, whirlpool, or steam room, you have to pay an extra unspecified fee each month.

We phoned the club in early August, nearly a month after the 48-hour deadline. A club employee told us the limited offer was still in effect. He also said the "additional fee" was $15 a month. All told, the price of the "free" two-year membership would add up to $558.

Near the end of November, we phoned the club again. At first, the employee who answered refused to discuss price over the phone; she said we'd have to come in and see a "counselor." When we persisted, we learned that the club's "limited" offer still hadn't reached its limit—some four and a half months after the 48-hour deadline.

—January 1991

Six of one . . .

Several readers spotted the funny math in this Dunkin' Donuts coupon. When you pay for a half dozen, they'll let you have six.

—February 1991

Another shady deal

A newspaper ad from the Drapery Depot in Escondido, California, offered a "threefer": two free window blinds for each one bought "at suggested retail price." In bold capital letters were the words "NO GIMMICKS-NO TRICKS."

But a teeny-print disclaimer at the bottom of the page certainly sounded a little gimmicky to us: "We never sell, or have ever sold at this so-called 'list' price . . . The term 'threefer' is used as an advertising hyperbole . . ."

—June 1990

A gotcha from the GOP

If you should receive a $25 check in the mail from the Republican Presidential Task Force in Washington, D.C., as did one of our staffers and several readers, read the small print on the back before you endorse and deposit the check. Your endorsement authorizes the Presidential Task Force to electronically withdraw $12.50 from your bank account each and every month, for the rest of your earthly days—or at least until you contact the Task Force or your bank to cancel the arrangement. Incidentally, you can't cancel for at least two months. That's to make sure the Task Force gets back its $25 investment.

The folder shown accompanied the check. It offers to "officially induct you into Who's Who in the Republican Party,"

alongside President Bush, Vice President Quayle, former President Nixon, and other GOP luminaries. That worthy publication is described as a "lasting record accessed and relied upon by commentators, media personalities, news makers, writers, elected officials. . . ." We bet it will be accessed and relied upon by compilers of mail-order lists as well.

How does one become worthy of such a singular honor? According to a certificate that donors receive, it's in recognition of "distinction and achievement in helping to promote and perpetuate the ideals and principles of the Republican Party."

The staffer who received this "Once in a Lifetime Opportunity" happens to be a Democrat.

—*November 1990*

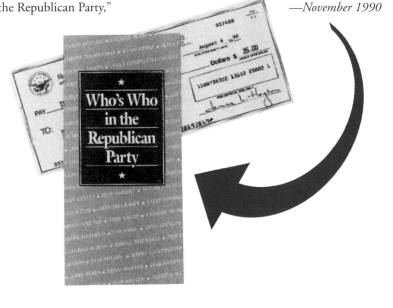

One small grocerie, please

A New York reader was generous enough to pass along this coupon for FREE GROCERIES. Look closely, and you'll see that it's good for up to 50 cents. Guess we won't be filling our shopping cart.

—September 1996

MANUFACTURER COUPON   EXPIRES 3/3/96

FREE GROCERIES (UP TO 50¢)
Excluding Tobacco, Alcohol, and Dairy Products.
when you buy one
Ortega® Product any variety
(except seasoning mix)

CONSUMER:
only on produ
will reimburse
ance with NE
10/91, availab
USA. Send c
Texas 88588-

Family matters

"**G**ood news!" a letter told *Consumer Reports* Production Manager Maggie Brenner. "Our new book, The Brenners Since the Civil War, is finally complete—and you, M. Brenner, are listed in it." The letter was signed by one George P. Brenner. That set us to wondering: Are the signers of these missives real people?

We called the number provided and asked for George Brenner. After momentary confusion, the customer-service representative gave us the story. George is a "Family Director," a real person who allows his name to be used in advertising but has no direct responsibility for the book. The book's publisher, Numa Corporation, which also does business as Halbert's, pays family directors a 2 percent commission on books sold through mailings directed to people with the same surname. So yes, Maggie, there is a George, though he's probably not a long-lost relative.

There was no relative's signature affixed to the family book pitch received by the San Fernando Valley Child Guidance Clinic, but it's worth a mention anyway. A letter addressed to Fernando V. San tried to sell the clinic a book on the San family in the U.S.

—July 1995

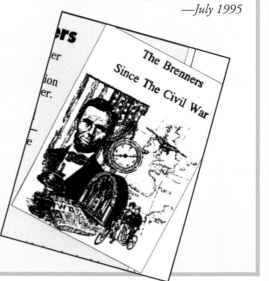

The Brenners Since The Civil War

☆ ☆ ☆ ☆ ☆ ☆ ☆ ☆ ☆ ☆ ☆ ☆ ☆ ☆ ☆ ☆ ☆ ☆ ☆

CHAPTER 7

FOOD FOLLIES

> *"[The new merchant] takes mustard that is just like anybody else's mustard, and he goes about saying, shouting, singing, chalking on walls, writing inside people's books, putting it everywhere, 'Smith's Mustard Is the Best.' And behold it is the Best!"*
>
> A character in the H. G. Wells novel *Tono-Bungay*

On the sides of houses used for important ceremonies, the Abelam of New Guinea have been said to post sacred designs called tambarans, representing the most powerful ancestral spirits of the tribe. A British anthropologist observed that magazines sometimes found their way into Abelam villages, and pages torn from them were duly posted. Favored pages were brightly colored food ads, he reported, "of the Spam and sweet corn and honey-baked ham type." Never having had the good fortune to see, much less eat, Spam, the Abelam had no idea what the pages offered, just that they were probably European tambarans and were therefore strong stuff.

Food labels and packages can prove nearly as mystifying here in the USA, despite clarifications from the Nutrition Labeling and Education Act of 1990. It required a new format for labeled nutrition information and defined claims. Without delving into the specifics of calcium-phosphorus ratios or requirements regarding Franklin Gothic Heavy type, here are the highlights:

- *Free.* The product must either be free of the nutrient in question or contain a dietetically trivial amount. Fat-free and sugar-free mean the food has less than 0.5 gram of each per serving; cholesterol-free means less than 2 milligrams; sodium-free means less than 5 milligrams.

- *Low.* As a rule, a food is low in a nutrient if a serving of that nutrient makes up 5 percent or less of the daily value. (The daily value for a good nutrient is a minimum amount recommended in a two-thousand-calorie-per-day diet; for a bad nutrient, it's a maximum.)

- *High, good source.* To qualify for a high claim—for example, "high in calcium"—food must contain 20 percent or more of the daily value for that nutrient per serving. "Good source" means a serving contains 10 to 19 percent of the daily value for the nutrient.

- *Lean.* Lean means that meat, poultry, or seafood has less than 10 grams of fat, less than 4 grams of saturated fat, and less than 95 milligrams of cholesterol per serving and per 100 grams.

- *Reduced, less, fewer, more, light.* Manufacturers who compare a nutritionally altered product with a regular product may use these words. The regular product, a.k.a. reference food, may be either an individual one (Lay's potato chips, say) or a group (the average nutrition of several leading potato chips). A relative claim must include the identity of the reference food and the percent difference. Reduced, less, and light (or lite) claims can't be made for products whose reference food already meets the requirement for a low claim. There's a lot more detail about more and less, but enough's enough. Let's move on to light.
  Light can mean one of two things: First, that a product contains one-third fewer calories or half the fat of the reference food. Second, that the sodium content of a low-calorie, low-fat food has been reduced by at least 50 percent. Light may describe color or texture, provided qualifying information is included. Names that have a long history of use, such as light brown sugar, can be used without qualifiers.

- *Healthy.* A healthy food must be low in fat and saturated fat and contain limited amounts of cholesterol and sodium. Some foods are also required to provide at least 10 percent of one or more nutrients.

- *Fresh.* When "fresh" is meant to suggest that a food is raw or unprocessed, it can be used only on food that is raw, has never been frozen or heated, and contains no preservatives. "Fresh frozen" can be used for foods that are quickly frozen while fresh.

- *Organic.* What gets this label? Crops grown without synthetic pesticides, meat from animals raised without antibiotics, and dairy cattle raised with access to pasture, for starters. Foods that have been irradiated or genetically engineered can't be labeled organic.

- *Natural.* According to the U.S. Food and Drug Administration, this word means that "nothing artificial or synthetic . . . has been included in or added to a food that would not normally be expected to be in the food. For its part, the U.S. Department of Agriculture says meat and poultry products labeled natural should contain no artificial ingredients, coloring ingredients, or chemical preservatives, and should have ingredients that are no more than minimally processed.

Aren't these rules about as clear as mud pie? No wonder a large chunk of submissions to the "Selling It" column consist of steamed-off juice labels, empty pretzel bags, squashed soda cans, and flattened cereal boxes. Judging by the questions that accompany these piles of packaging, the trio of fat, calories, and sugar can be especially befuddling. (Q: Can ice cream shot through with cookie dough, chips, or candy really be low-fat? A: Yes, but the inclusions often hike calories and sugar.)

A 1997 survey by *Food Marketing Institute and Prevention* magazine confirmed that fat content and calories are the figures America's label readers look for first. However, when it comes to nutrition, the gap between what people say and what they do can be as wide as a BarcaLounger. In the tug-of-war between our respect for foods that will make us svelte and our lust for foods that will make us fat, lust is winning at the moment. According to Mintel's Global New Products Database, food makers have been introducing fewer and fewer reduced-fat products: 2,076 in 1996; 1,405 in 1997; 1,180 in 1998; and 481 in 1999 (although the number rose to 1,057 in 2000).

Food packages can confuse in plenty of other ways, too. They can:

- *Suggest ingredients that aren't there.* Labels for Aunt Fanny's Apple Sweet Roll and Mrs. Wright's Apple Sweet Roll each mentioned more than twenty-five ingredients. Not one was apple. The Real Key Lime Pound Cake contained no key lime or other lime: The closest thing to a citrus fruit listed was orange oil. Davis Butter Rolls listed no butter. Crunchy Cheez Doodles were said to have "Oodles of real cheese." However, the package indicated that the Doodles' salt weighed about .02 ounce, and the ingredients listed cheese *after* salt, so cheese must have weighed less than .02 ounce. Since oodles was plural, one oodle must have weighed less than .01 ounce.

Some companies even "inboard" the name of a desirable ingredient into the brand name. Aunt Maple's Syrup listed no maple syrup. And some companies ignore ingredients that *are* there. A product called Kave Kure was "all cheese," but in addition to aged cheddar cheese, it consisted of whey, water, cream, salt, dextrose, guar gum, sorbic acid, citric acid, and artificial color.

Officially, a food is misbranded if its labeling is false and misleading in any particular. If the FDA receives complaints, it will examine the entire label and note whether or not a word in the name is indeed represented by, say, artificial flavors.

- *Use a name that's merely an image.* Campbell's used to sell soups it called Manhandlers, implying that they were hearty enough to feed a half-starved lumberjack. But apparently, as "Selling It" noted in 1980, the company discovered there were more dieters than ravenous outdoorsmen. So it began a new campaign, the Light Ones, for a line of soups with 90 calories or fewer per serving. At least one of the Light Ones, vegetable beef, turned out to be a former Manhandler.

- *Be off in their numbers.* Nutrient analyses can be off by up to 20 percent, to allow for natural variations in food. As a result, a half cup of ice cream that claims 270 calories per serving could actually supply anywhere from 216 to 324 calories. Calories can also be rounded—to the nearest 5-calorie increment if the food has 50 calories or less; to the nearest 10-calorie increment if the food has more than 50 calories.

- *Make claims for one that are true for all.* These are known as pre-emptive claims, and they got their start around the turn of the last century, when Schlitz Beer began boasting that its bottles were "washed with live steam." So were other beer bottles, but no other company had thought to make the claim. More recently, such so-what claims have included "no cholesterol" (for vegetable products like peanut butter) and "fat-free" (for salsa). The FDA says that foods that are "born" without a certain bad ingredient must be labeled to indicate that *all* foods of that type meet the claim. For example, a fat-free claim on applesauce has to read "applesauce, a fat-free food."

- *Do a juice switcheroo.* Ocean Spray Cranberry and Key Lime Premium Juice declares itself 100 percent juice but not 100 percent cranberry and key lime; the first two juices listed are grape and apple. Companies generally explain that 100 percent of some juices (like cranberry) wouldn't taste so great, or that some juices are very expensive (apple juice is fairly cheap and is often used in greater quantity than others).

Products that claim to contain juice are supposed to declare the total percentage of juice on their information panel. Those with less than 100 percent juice are supposed to call themselves something other than juice—beverage, drink, cocktail, or juice blend, for instance.

- *Suggest a weird serving size.* Before the labeling act, serving sizes were up to the manufacturer and could make little sense. Years ago, for instance, "Selling It" featured crab meat whose package shrank from 8 ounces to 6. The new, smaller package continued to insist that buyers would get two servings from it; the company simply reduced the serving size from 4 ounces to 3.

  Today, serving sizes are based on FDA lists of "Reference Amounts Customarily Consumed Per Eating Occasion." A serving of cookies, for instance, is as close as the maker can get to the reference amount of 30 grams without breaking cookies into crumbs: If each cookie in a package weighs 13 grams, a serving is two cookies.

  That sounds sensible, but some sizes still require fairly fancy slicing and dicing. Not long ago, a frozen-fish company was offering "4 Breaded Fish Portions." The serving size was "3 fish portions"; the servings per container "about 2."

- *Use cute terms that mean little.* In the late 1980s, *Consumer Reports*' Staffer In Charge of Pouring and Sifting Things counted the number of raisins in Kellogg's Raisin Bran, to find out just how many are in those "two scoops" of which Kellogg is so proud. He found 565 raisins per box on average, versus 323 for Post Raisin Bran, the main competition. On the other hand, Kellogg's raisins were smaller than Post's.

- *Use words that confuse.* Healthful-sounding brown "wheat" breads may lack the grain's beneficial bran and germ and may not have much dietary fiber. As of 2001, Home Pride Butter Top Wheat bread had 0 grams of fiber per slice.

  In 1984, we reported on popcorn made by Wileswood Inc. that included "real artificial coloring." More recently, we've seen Pepperidge Farm Fudge Striped Chocolate Chunk cookies with "Only Real Ingredients" and Albertson's "100% Real Margarine." But our favorite words that confuse are euphemisms. It took a little pondering to realize that "beef oil" was rendered beef fat.

Faced with such butchery of the English language, one can only applaud the straightforward message sent to customers of a Chinese food supplier, one of whom was a *Consumer Reports* subscriber:

Dear Sir, The ingredients of our products [include] chilli paste with garlic. . . . The germinating seeds of chilli may look like worms while the skin of garlic may look like the wings of insects. Our barbecue sauce contains small dried shrimps whose feet may look like those of some insects. We hope this clarifies the doubts and your kind attention will be much appreciated. > > >

Also contains viscous bee fluid

Trader Joe's Honey Nut O's may have no preservatives and no artificial ingredients, but in its quest for a healthful image, the cereal also boasts one of the more amusing euphemisms we've seen recently: Following whole oat flour in the list of ingredients is "crystallized evaporated cane juice." A customer-service representative at Trader Joe's confirmed our suspicions. It's sugar. For the record, the representative pointed out that it's less refined than "regular" sugar and has a higher mineral content. Says one of our staff food experts: "Sugar is sugar, and the trace minerals would not make a meaningful difference."

—*March 1997*

Mmmm. Tastes like . . . red

The reader who bought these fruit-flavored Starburst candy canes last Christmas had no problem with orange, strawberry, and lemon flavors. But green?

—*November 1999*

Preheat torch to 950°

When it comes to cooking, convenience sells. Unfortunately, the convenience claims food companies cook up aren't always as advertised. Take Michael Angelo's Gourmet Italian Foods Eggplant Parmesan. "Ready in just 5 minutes," reads a seal on the package. But a California reader noted that the cooking instructions call for a total of 30 to 45 minutes in a microwave or 70 to 85 minutes in a conventional oven, plus an hour of thawing and 5 to 10 minutes of cooling off, either way. "Perhaps they forgot to include the blow-torch method," our reader suggested.

"What they're really meaning there," explained a Michael Angelo spokesperson, "is five minutes per portion. Maybe we should change the wording a little bit."

Another reader sent us a bag of True Value Frozen Blackeyed Peas. Conveniently "microwaveable," the front of the bag proclaims. Not so fast, says the back: "These are best cooked by conventional methods due to the nature of Blackeyed Peas." Undaunted unconventional cooks are invited to write the company's consumer service department in Oklahoma for microwave instructions. So, given the mailing time involved, conveniently microwaving the peas should take only two weeks or so.

—*January 1993*

—*July 1999*

Orange juice squeezes out a victory

Let's see. A cup of Tropicana Season's Best Calcium orange juice has 300 milligrams of calcium, the label says, and a cup of skim milk has 302 milligrams. Last time we checked, 302 was more than 300. So, in a carton sent us last spring, why was the bar graph longer for Season's Best? Good question. In a carton we bought this summer, milk had gained its rightful place.

—October 1999

Ye olde shortbreade

Guess a tradition has to start somewhere.
—July 1999

But "mango" rhymes

Mango Tropitango is a tangy and sweet real fruit treat, the label says. So the dried fruit inside is mango? Don't be silly. The fruit is . . . pineapple. The flavor is mango. Artificial mango.

—June 1999

INGREDIENTS: DRIED THAILAND PINEAPPLE (CONTAINS SUGAR, ARTIFICIAL COLORING, ARTIFICIAL MANGO FLAVOR). SULFUR DIOXIDE ADDED AS A PRESERVATIVE.

What's in a name?

A reader noticed something funny about Dassänt's New England Pumpkin Spice Bread & Muffin Mix: It has no pumpkin. Dassänt's Hood River Apple Spice Cake & Muffin Mix? Yup. No apple. You add those yourself. Moreover, the two mixes list the same ingredients, in the same order. A customer-service representative confirmed that the mixes are "basically the same," and gave us permission to put pumpkin in the apple mix, as long as we followed directions on the pumpkin box. "Gosh," notes our reader, "maybe they should call it New England Pumpkin, Cranberry & Walnut Spice Bread & Muffin Mix. Then they'd suck in the cranberry and walnut lovers . . . without adding a thing to the mix inside!" We didn't have the heart to ask the company what New England and Hood River had to do with anything.

—February 1999

Maybe "Rice Soup" sounded too weird

Why did the chicken cross the road? So it wouldn't end up in Buckeye Beans & Herbs Chick'n Rice Soup, apparently. Once you get to the other side of the package, you find that it's 100 per cent poultry-free: no chicken, no chicken broth. You add those, plus six other items.

—July 1998

Bring your own broccoli

Concord Foods' Cream of Broccoli Soup Mix has wheat flour, disodium inosinate, lecithin, and a wealth of other ingredients. But you won't find broccoli, even dried, among them. That's for you to add (along with milk and butter).

—June 1997

My stingy Valentine

The serving size of Dove Truffle Hearts, according to the labeled Nutrition Facts: "4 pieces." The servings per box: "about 3." It seems reasonable to conclude that there are 12 chocolates inside. But a description elsewhere mentions 8 pieces. Which is right? Only the foil insert reveals the answer.

—July 1997

Mistaken identity?

These Pepperidge Farm cookies look like twins. Both are raspberry and come twelve to the package, both are the same size, both claim to be natural or to have no artificial ingredients, both have 120 calories per serving with three grams of total fat, both are cholesterol-free, and both start off with the same ingredients —flour and riboflavin (after that, the ingredients vary slightly; we guess they're fraternal twins). So why is one labeled "reduced fat" while the other isn't, and why does that reduced-fat package cost 20 cents more than the other—$2.39 versus $2.19? We found out, but it wasn't easy.

A representative at Pepperidge Farm's comments line suggested that most reduced-fat products simply cost a little more but that "no one could give you a definitive answer." Not taking "no one" for an answer, we called the company's public-relations office, where an employee told us she couldn't say why one cookie costs more than another.

At last, we reached a vice president for corporate communications and learned the answers, along with a bit about selling cookies: (1) Chantilly claims reduced fat because it has slightly less fat than Fruitful; nutrition numbers are rounded. (2) Chantilly costs more because its somewhat different formula requires a slower production line. (3) Both survive in the marketplace because some consumers want a better-for-you product in a green package—Chantilly—and others don't. "Fruitful," said the VP, "speaks to the person who just wants a fruity cookie."

For the record, our sensory experts said the cookies are taste-alikes, too. Most people would notice no difference.

—*October 1997*

Something to crow about?

On-Cor's Dumplings & Chicken dinner, its label boasts, isn't made with just any chicken but with "NATURAL CHICKEN!" A Pennsylvania reader asked what unnatural chicken might be, so we called On-Cor. A representative explained that the dinner has "all-real chicken," not chicken loaf.

—April 1997

The real deal

In April, we featured a frozen dinner of "NATURAL CHICKEN!"—which the maker told us meant "real" chicken, not chicken loaf. Now a reader has sent us Betty Crocker's Fettuccine Alfredo Hamburger Helper, "made with real ingredients."

—June 1997

Seeing double

Sure you can have a sliver this big. But if you do, you'll be eating two servings, says a small note under this ad for Kraft's Philadelphia Free Cream Cheese.

—October 1995

Cheesecake contains 2.5 grams of fat per serving. Two servings shown.

Now you can have a Sliver this Big.

Introducing New PHILLY® FREE®.

Cheesecake contains 2.5 grams of fat per serving. Two servings shown.

We're waiting for wheat-germ Twinkies

A Virginia reader blinked recently when he spied a package of Hostess Oat Bran Muffins. Could it be that Hostess, home of the HoHo and other nutritionally challenged confections, had begun selling health food? Nah. Below, nutrition figures from the muffins and from Hostess Cupcakes. We invite you to match the numbers to the product (answer below).

Calories 320	Calories 330
Fat calories 140	Fat calories 100
Total fat 15 g.	Total fat 11 g.
Saturated fat 2 g.	Saturated fat 5 g.
Cholesterol 0 mg.	Cholesterol 5 mg.
Sodium 290 mg.	Sodium 520 mg.
Carbohydrates 43 g.	Carbohydrates 56 g.
Fiber 2 g.	Fiber 2 g.

—September 1995

(Muffins on left; Cupcakes on right)

Look, but don't eat

I ntrigued by the artistic pizza advertised by Reno's Airport Plaza Hotel? Don't get too interested. It may be "so good, you'll never try theirs again," but you'll never know. A little note at the bottom of the menu says, "Pizza shown not available."

—August 1995

Not so fast

"**R**eady in seconds." Well, we guess that's true. The back of the package reveals the cooking time to be—let's see—600 to 720 seconds in a pan; 120 to 180 in a microwave oven.

—*July 1995*

Talking turkey

Guess what color meat you get in Honeysuckle White ground turkey, billed as "light and healthy," with "more of what you like." Right. Mostly dark.

—*June 1995*

Is this as clear as consommé?

"**H**earty" soup sounds m'm m'm good on a chilly day, as marketers well know, but just what does hearty mean? We called the consumer line at four of the big names in soup and collected the following definitions:

Lipton: "Hearty certainly relates to the body of the soup and to the predominance of noodles. The soup may be heavier in weight. It has to do with flavor, and type and amount of noodles. Spices, too."

Campbell's: "It has to do with the size of the vegetables. A hearty soup is closer to a stew. It's a slight difference, nothing dramatic. You might not notice the difference unless you were looking for it."

Knorr: "A regular soup would be maybe vegetable or hot and sour—more of the broth types. For instance, French onion, I don't consider hearty. In my opinion, it's the availability of extra ingredients, and maybe hearty soup is a little thicker."

Progresso: "It's just kind of a word they use as far as describing soup with ingredients that are nutritious. A lot of your pasta soups have it. It's more or less the amount of vegetables. It's kind of a PR, go-getter type thing."

So now you know.

—*May 1995*

Now we're cooking

A California reader who took these hash browns on a camping trip was happy to read "No Cooking Required" on the front of the package. After a long hike, she took out the package and noticed that the back told a different story: Boil water, add the contents, let the mix stand for five minutes, drain it, then fry it in a hot greased pan until brown. "If that isn't cooking," she wrote, "I'll eat my shoe."

—January 1995

Yes, we have no potatoes

A Texas reader was enjoying a can of Alimentco's Krunchy Potato Sticks, Pizza Flavor, when he noticed something odd. Although the ingredients include everything from annatto extract to whey protein concentrate, a certain starchy tuber was absent.

—October 1994

And have some diet soda with dessert

G reat. A recipe using no-fat, no-cholesterol Egg Beaters. Guess we'll use no-fat, no-cholesterol ground chuck when we make that meatloaf.

—February 1994

What happened to oil and vinegar?

"**A**pparently," a Maryland reader notes, "that old family [established 1811, the label says] had access to some mighty sophisticated ingredients." What? Didn't everyone's great-great-grandmother cook with propylene glycol alginate?

—*December 1993*

Duddy buddies

"**I** am sure," a reader wrote, "that the chocolate chips and peanut butter are quite flavorful, but I did not know that Glad Lock Zipper Bags improved the flavor of anything. It seems to me that this 'All-Star ingredient' would be just a little too chewy for most people's tastes." He suggested aluminum foil as an easier-to-swallow alternative.

—*November 1993*

A little black lie

The California Olive Industry wants to set you straight about its product. "Contrary to what you may believe," says its ad from the pages of *Eating Well* magazine, "California Ripe Olives are not high in fat AND they are cholesterol free." They're right about the cholesterol, but a little slippery on the fat. As the ad explains, one olive contains approximately one gram of fat and only nine calories. Since one gram of fat has nine calories, all the calories in an olive come from fat, which hardly makes it a low-fat food.

True, adding a few olives to your pasta (the half-plate shown below accompanied the ad) won't put you over the recommended intake of fat—no more than 30 percent of your caloric intake. But tossing in 14 olives (the number that would show if a full plate were pictured) would add the amount of fat in one and a half cups of whole milk or about twenty-five potato chips. Like other high-fat foods, olives should be eaten in moderation.

—*October 1993*

Is this fish worth its (low) salt?

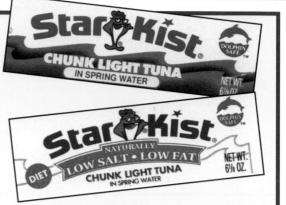

What's the difference between Star-Kist Chunk Light Tuna in Spring Water and Star-Kist Diet Chunk Light Tuna in Spring Water? One word and 80 cents, a reader from Indiana assumed. As he pointed out, the fat content of the two products is the same, and the "diet" tuna's label lists five more calories per serving than the other type. But our reader paid $1.69 for the diet can; 89 cents for the other.

When we checked with Star-Kist, an official said that "all tuna in spring water is a naturally low-fat food," and that the calorie count for any can of tuna may vary slightly. "The key thing," she said, is that the diet product has less sodium— 100 milligrams per serving, versus 250 milligrams. She explained that types of tuna with a naturally low sodium content are hand picked—"a very labor-intensive process" that accounts for diet tuna's higher cost. (Our own food experts suspect that the fish's saltiness has less to do with its type than with the solutions used in processing.)

To trim fat off your food bill and salt from your diet, buy the cheaper tuna and rinse it with tap water, which will flush away much of the excess salt.

—*July 1993*

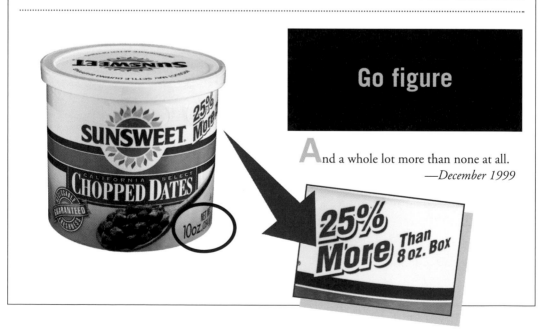

Go figure

And a whole lot more than none at all.
—*December 1999*

Double talk

Stop the presses! A 14-ounce pot pie has twice as much chicken as a 7-ounce pie.

—April 1993

The flesh is weak

A consumer concerned about weight might well have been drawn to a coupon good for a free two-liter bottle of diet Coke. A six-ounce serving of diet Coke does save you calories (it has 71 fewer than a serving of Coca-Cola Classic). But to qualify for the free diet soda, you have to buy Fisher mixed nuts (170 calories per serving), Duncan Hines cookies (110 calories per serving), and Pringles potato chips (170 calories per serving).

—October 1991

Fred mired

An Idaho reader sent us this Fred Meyer recipe from the back of a box of Fred Meyer Crisp Crunch cereal, a product of Oregon-based Fred Meyer Inc.

We think we've spotted an opening for Fred in the baking-powder business.

—February 1993

Fred Meyer Crisp Crunch K
Vitamin Fortified Sweetened Cereal

CRISPY RAISIN COOKIES

½ cup Fred Meyer vegetable shortening
½ cup packed Fred Meyer brown sugar
1 Fred Meyer egg
1 teaspoon Fred Meyer vanilla extract
1 cup Fred Meyer all-purpose flour
1 teaspoon baking powder
1 teaspoon Fred Meyer cinnamon
⅛ teaspoon Fred Meyer salt
2½ cups Fred Meyer Crisp Crunch cereal
¾ cup Fred Meyer raisins

Dinnertime

Pictured here is the front label from Snak Club Old Fashion Red Licorice. We were charmed by its slogan, "A meal in itself." Who needs the basic food groups when you can dine on corn syrup, wheat flour, citric acid, and artificial flavor and color?

—March 1992

Snak Club
OLD FASHION
RED LICORICE
NET WT. 5 OZ.   A MEAL IN ITSELF   142 GRAMS

Delicious? Maybe. Nutritious? Read on.

Part of the fun for people who read food labels is digesting the hyperbole that often surrounds the nutrition information. Looking at a jar of Wheat Nuts, a snack made by AnaCon Foods, a label addict discovers that the ridged nuggets inside are a "deliciously unique blend of wholesome ingredients specially prepared for today's nutrition-conscious consumer." That sounds good.

But then the label reader notices that Wheat Nuts have 200 calories per one-ounce serving. Not so good. Worse still, they contain 19 grams of fat (from partially hydrogenated soybean oil) per ounce, which means that more than 85 percent of their calories come from fat. That's almost half again as much fat as potato chips have. Even peanuts get only 74 percent of their calories from fat.

No one should expect a snack food to be completely without sin. But is today's nutrition-conscious consumer any less worried about fat than yesterday's?

—November 1991

Name-dropping

Pictured is a box of what you'd be forgiven for calling Kellogg's NBC Crispix. It offers a *Tonight Show with Jay Leno* T-shirt on the top, bottom, and side panels; lists three of "Jay's Jokes"; calls Crispix and *The Tonight Show* a "Great Nighttime Mix"; and displays a big photo of Leno. With all that offering, joking, and mixing going on, it's easy to miss the teensy type that says "No Celebrity Endorsement Implied."

When we asked Kellogg what Leno was doing if not endorsing, we were told that Kellogg has an agreement with NBC, not with Leno himself, and that Kellogg isn't claiming the comedian makes a habit of munching Crispix. So we guess what Leno is doing is smiling at the prospect of people wearing his T-shirt, telling his jokes, watching his show—and eating anything they please.

—February 1994

How sweet it is

No cereal maker likes to admit that its product is almost half sugar. Particularly not Kellogg's, with its big seller Corn Pops—the cereal that used to be called Sugar Pops.

Nowadays, the Corn Pops box takes the offensive on its side panel with an educational essay on nutrition, titled "A Good Breakfast . . . What's It Mean?" A handy bar graph shows that a one-ounce serving of Corn Pops has a good deal less sugar than an apple, a banana, or two pancakes with syrup.

One problem with this information is that many people would eat more than a one-ounce serving of the cereal. Another is that comparing a bowl of cereal to a piece of fruit is comparing apples and orangutans.

Needless to say, Kellogg's hasn't compared a serving of Sugar . . . uh, Corn Pops to a serving of a more nutritious cereal you might give your child. Cheerios, for instance, has about one-tenth the sugar of Corn Pops, and provides more fiber and protein than the sugar-laden, vitamin-injected cereal.

The side panel also sports Kellogg's recommendation for a good breakfast: Corn Pops with milk, juice, toast, and a glass of milk. That would be a pretty good breakfast—but even better if you substituted a more nutritious cereal for the Corn Pops.

—*March 1991*

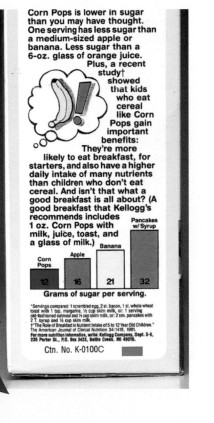

★ ☆ ★ ☆ ★ ☆ ★ ☆ ★ ☆ ★ ☆ ★ ☆ ★ ☆ ★ ☆ ★ ☆ ★ ☆ ★ ☆ ★ ☆ ★ ☆ ★

CHAPTER 8

YOU MAY ALREADY HAVE LOST

"Sometimes I get mighty mad at advertising—tempting me all the time. I wish it would leave me be."

Andy Consumer, typical American,
created in the 1920s by a humor magazine

It's soooo tempting to get something for nothing. What else could account for the behavior of an eighty-three-year-old woman who ordered five truckloads of magazines, figurines, videotapes, and other goodies from sweepstakes companies—in the belief, no doubt, that ordering would boost her chances of winning. She had subscribed to *Farm Living,* though she was not from the country and didn't farm; *Outdoor Photographer,* though she was not a photographer; and *Black Men's Quarterly,* though she was neither African-American nor a man. Her son and daughter-in-law became suspicious when they noticed that her financial account was down $51,000.

An eighty-eight-year-old California man—recipient of an American Family Publishers promotion that said, "You're our newest $11 million winner"—flew to Tampa because he thought he could collect his sweepstakes winnings there. (The mailing had a Tampa return address.) He had plenty of company from other "winners" who wandered around Tampa International Airport looking for Ed McMahon. They thought he'd be there to meet them.

A Senate committee investigating sweepstakes in 1999 heard about a woman who was trying to settle the estate of her late father-in-law. She found he had amassed seventeen boxes of solicitations and had, through one sweepstakes sponsor, renewed two magazine subscriptions through the year 2086.

Sweepstakes mailings go to virtually every home in America and have gained the companies that mail them millions on millions of dollars in profits over the years. But they've also generated lots of losses. A *Consumer Reports* sampling of cases from federal and state agencies suggested that hundreds of thousands of consumers, often elderly, have been bilked out of at least tens of millions of dollars a year. During 2000, the Federal Trade Commission received more than eleven thousand complaints about sweepstakes and prize and gift promotions.

In February 2000, a Publishers Clearing House spokesman was quoted as saying, "We're no different than a store that hangs out a sign that said, 'Come into our store.' Our store is our envelope." The attorney general of Texas had a different opinion. In filing suit against the company in 1999, he noted that sweepstakes mailings are "letter bombs, filled with deception." That may be going a little too far, given that entering an occasional sweepstakes can be fun if it's above-board (even Consumers Union runs a raffle to raise funds, and *Consumer Reports* is offered by Publishers Clearing House). Still, it pays to know what come-ons you'll encounter.

The process often starts with a "pre-alert"—a mailing that generates excitement for the sweepstakes package to come. *Reader's Digest* pioneered this technique in the 1980s. Often the pre-alert looks as if it's been mailed by a third party—say, Citizens State Bank of Clara City, Minnesota. Business cards may be included to lend an appearance of personal contact—an appearance that could dissipate on closer inspection. Cards from *Reader's Digest,* for example, don't have real contact information; they just list the company's city, state, and zip code. "Also, most legitimate business cards don't have document codes printed in the upper right-hand corner," the trade publication *Inside Direct Mail* notes helpfully, "but the average consumer might not notice."

After the opening gambit, companies use various gimmicks to get you to respond. Among them:

- *The important document.* You'll see notices like "security seal," "monitored delivery," "confidential," "important message," "tamper proof," "contents need immediate attention"—all of that is hoo-hah. If mail is sent with bulk postage, you haven't won anything. If you hit the big one, you'll likely hear by certified, overnight, or, at the very least, first-class mail.

- *The "involvement device."* It could be a stamp, a token, a rub-off, a sealed envelope, maybe even a jigsaw puzzle—whatever gets you to interact with the offer.

- *The fine print.* Small, scrunched, poor-quality type makes some rules easy to miss.

- *The next level.* Forget about such warnings as "level 4 alert." You need enter only once to have a chance to win a legitimate sweepstakes. Entrants aren't weeded out as the contest progresses.

- *The check.* A fake check must carry a statement that it's not a negotiable instrument and has no cash value. Sometimes that statement is buried.

- *The 900 phone number.* You can call (and pay several dollars) just to find out that the fake check can't be cashed.

- *The order form.* It could make you think you have to order to win. You don't, but you may have to turn the page over and read tiny type to find that out.

- *The government document.* Beware of eagles, official-sounding groups, and pulse-quickeners like "Urgent!" Check for a little disclaimer like "not affiliated with the U.S. Government."

- *The affidavit.* Judicial folderol—engravings of robed ladies toting scales, for instance—makes some sweepstakes entries look as if they've come from law firms.

- *The inflated term.* In 1987, a company called Continental Marketing and Research wrote to *Consumer Reports.* "We are pleased to permit you to claim ownership of the revolutionary new Kamasura Model 250 VRX Motor Cycle," the letter said. Our dreams of taking to the open road were dashed when we learned that the cycle was a moped with what amounted to a chain-saw engine. To claim it, we would have had to pay more than $300.

- *The obvious observation.* A *Reader's Digest* letter said, "According to statistical estimates, by returning your Computer Cards IMMEDIATELY, no other entry will have a better chance of claiming that TWO MILLION DOLLARS." No kidding. No other entry will have a worse chance, either.

Such tricks have not gone unnoticed by federal and state agencies, which use various laws to prosecute bad apples. The legislation that's most recent and largest in scope is the Deceptive Mail Prevention and Enforcement Act, signed by President Clinton in December 1999. It imposes restrictions on most sweepstakes-entry materials sent via U.S. mail. Among other requirements, the act says that mailings, rules, and entry forms must show: that no purchase is necessary to enter, and that a purchase won't improve your chances of winning; the estimated odds of winning; the quantity, estimated retail value, and nature of each prize; the schedule of any payments; and the name, address, and phone number of the company sponsoring the contest. In addition, you must be able to have your name removed from the company's mailing list. The law also forbids using envelopes that mimic government mailings. Civil penalties for breaking regulations range up to $1 million; if the Postal Service has obtained a stop order, fines for violating it go as high as $2 million.

Other laws that govern contests include the FTC's Telemarketing Sales Rule, which requires telemarketers offering a sweepstakes to note that no purchase is needed to enter and to disclose the odds of receiving a prize. Federal and state deceptive-trade laws also prohibit companies from tricking people into making a purchase.

Recent suits focused on American Family Enterprises (in charge of the American Family Publishers sweepstakes, formerly plugged by Dick Clark and Mr. McMahon), Publishers Clearing House, and Reader's Digest. In 1999 American Family Enterprises agreed to a $33 million settlement of lawsuits claiming that consumers were lured into buying magazines and other products because they thought they'd increase their chances of winning. The settlement covered up to thirty-five million people. By that time, however, American Family had filed for Chapter 11 bankruptcy protection.

More recently, Publishers Clearing House has been hit repeatedly. In 2000, a federal judge approved a $30 million settlement of a class-action suit against the company (brought, again, on behalf of consumers who thought that buying magazines would better their chances). And in 2001, the company agreed to pay $34 million in a deal with 26 states.

Meanwhile, Reader's Digest agreed to pay more than $6 million to settle allegations that its promotions misled customers in 32 states and Washington, D.C.

To add to their woes, the big names in sweepstakes have had their reputations besmirched by impostors. In 1997 six people pretended they were with Publishers Clearing House when calling elderly people in eight states. They told victims they'd won the grand prize—if they prepaid federal income tax on the prize money. The impostors often promised the victims that Ed McMahon would deliver the prize and take them to lunch. (Mr. McMahon, of course, worked for PCH's competition—and you'd think the miscreants could at least have offered dinner.) The perpetrators were charged with conspiracy to commit wire fraud.

In 1979, some *Consumer Reports* readers received a notice from "Contest Clearing House" saying that their entry had been received and they could take a vacation in Florida. A phone number was appended. The readers had never sent an entry, and the number was long-distance. A call revealed that accommodations and coupons were free, but food, transportation, taxes, and other fees were not—and there would be "an interesting land sales presentation" for the vacationer to attend.

In the 1990s, Family Publishers Clearing Center and Publishers Award Bureau were asking consumers to fork over several hundred dollars to be eligible for an award—almost always, the FTC said, a "building lot." The lot proved to be nothing more than a license to use land in Baja California accessible only by off-road vehicles and lacking water and electricity.

Consumers may be getting wary of mailed come-ons, but their interest in sweepstakes web sites is on the rise.

Play if you want, but do so with your eyes open. Here are some tips:

- First, know what you're entering. You may think all those "You've Won!" contests are sweepstakes, but technically there are a few different types. In a sweepstakes, you get a chance to win a prize without having to answer any questions or pay anything. The winner is chosen by chance. In a skill contest, you must answer a question or pass a test, and a winner isn't chosen by chance. You may have to pay an entry fee or buy something. In a lottery, you pay to have a chance at winning a prize. Lotteries are legal only if they're run by a state or by certain charities.
- Winners don't have to provide a credit card number, send money, call a 900 phone number, or "make a small purchase."
- Be suspicious of phone calls, e-mails, or letters saying you've won a prize when you don't remember entering a contest.
- A "free" trip may be a lure to a sales presentation for a time-share, or might require you to pay some expenses in advance.
- If you receive any prize, it may be negligible. A *Consumer Reports* editor's "Tiffany Diamond Pendant," awarded after he and his wife drove to a resort and listened to a long pitch, was worth $15.
- Hunt for the odds of winning.
- Know that if you choose to receive a lump-sum prize in a state lottery, you often get less than half the jackpot whose full value is trumpeted. The lump sum is the amount it would take to invest now to guarantee payment of the full amount over time. In a recent $141 million California lottery, for instance, the lump-sum payment was about $43 million: $70.8 million (the amount the state would need to invest now to guarantee the full amount in 26 annual payments), minus taxes.
- Never enter a foreign lottery.

Finally, although it's tempting to feel special when you're addressed by name and called a winner, resist the urge. After all, these people don't really know you. A mail-order outfit called Spencer Gifts once sent *Consumer Reports* a $50,000 super-prize sweepstakes entry ticket along with a free medical emergency card. The mailing was addressed to Mrs. Consumers Union. The name embossed on the card: Mr. Nsumers Union of th. > > >

A wheeler-dealer

"This shall serve as our final notification regarding a fully detailed 1997 model car we will deliver directly to you," says the top sheet below, from Millennium Sales of West Palm Beach, Florida. "Failure to respond by the posted deadline date will nullify your opportunity to claim the $15,638.00 Automobile. Failure to respond will result in forfeiture of the 1997 model car pending delivery to you." On another sheet is a list of six cars, from a Mustang GT to a Chevy Blazer. You're supposed to choose the one you want and send $21.99 to guarantee delivery.

On the back of a third sheet, hidden in a fog of pale gray type, is a surprise. There are actually two cars involved here. One, a 1997 Chevy Camaro worth $15,638, is the grand prize in a sweepstakes. The second is a 1997 model car. Get it? Perhaps we haven't put the emphasis in the right place. It's a model car. "This is a nationwide promotional offer," the gray type says, "by [a] sponsor whose purpose is to promote the sale of selected 1997 1:39 scale model cars."

A translation of the carefully worded notification above: Respond by the deadline to enter the sweepstakes and have a chance at the big car; send a check for $21.99 and receive a little car. "I know these offers are a dime a dozen," writes the reader who received this one, "but this truly is one of the more deceptive ones I've seen. And I'm in advertising."

—*November 1997*

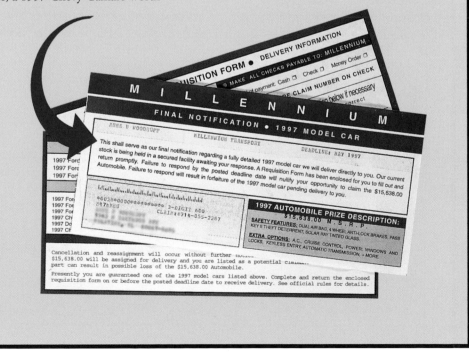

Several readers have called our attention to the selling tactics of Suarez Corporation Industries, which are so ingeniously misleading they deserve a broader audience. Last year, Suarez—which does business as Lindenwold Fine Jewelers and twenty or so other names—sent a New Jersey reader four mailings within a few weeks. Here's a sampler of SCI strategies.

February 22: A letter tells the reader he has won a major national sweepstakes and should expect important documents.

February 24: A nine-piece mailing repeats that our reader is a winner. "There are many misleading prize giveaways that require some type of payment from winners," it points out helpfully. "Beware of such sweepstakes." Then come the gotchas.

Before our reader's "cash claim eligibility" can be registered, he must be awarded his Finalist prize, a one-carat "cubic zirconium diamond" (in other words, a diamond that's not a diamond). It happens that this gem has already been mounted, so our reader can show it off immediately. But—whoops—sweepstakes rules award only the diamond, not the mounting. "To patch up this confusion," the letter states, Lindenwold will let our reader choose a mounting from those pictured in an enclosed brochure. He need only "cover the standard $19 Transfer Deposit Fee."

The mailing includes a couple of "handwritten" notes and an estimate of the cost of a real diamond in a similar setting. It shows that, for his $19, our

reader gets a fake diamond ring that, if it were real, would cost $3,500. A Certificate of Authenticity describes the quality of this "pure cubic zirconia," using such gemspeak as table, girdle, and culet.

March 10: A notice from Lindenwold's Board of Compensation and Property Endowment tells our reader to expect "verification and release documents" within forty-eight hours. "You may feel free to notify your immediate family and friends that you have won a cash prize," the notice says.

March 15: Our reader wins more gems that have already been set. Again, there's that pesky mounting fee. This time, there's also a letter typed on onionskin paper, purportedly from a Dutch gem expert who has examined the prize. According to scrawled notes at the top of the page, the letter has been translated from Dutch to English for a fee of 3.4 pounds. Perhaps that explains the man-from-Mars phraseology: "Greetings, I have been pleasured today with the good news of your winnings in the Nationale [sic] Publicity Sweepstakes." Our reader, who refused all offers, was especially tickled by the company names used by Suarez/Lindenwold. The sweepstakes notification came from a Lindenwold division called Earnst and Alexander Holding Associates (no, not Ernst and Young, a well-known accounting firm, or Alexander and Alexander, an insurance broker). Another mailing came from Case, Waterman and Associates, based in the Edgar Price Professional

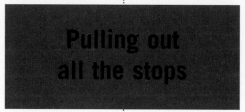

Pulling out all the stops

Building (no, not Price, Waterhouse, another big name in accounting). And the Dutch assessment of the gems' worth? It came from an "international purveyor of fine diamonds and gem stones" known as DeVoorst (no, not De Beers).

According to the Better Business Bureau, Suarez Corporation Industries has responded to consumers' complaints by offering a refund or providing a reasonable explanation. Nevertheless, there have been several attempts to make SCI change the way it does business. In February, the company (without admitting guilt) settled a U.S. Postal Service complaint that its schemes constituted an illegal lottery. That consent decree should prevent it from using some of the tactics it used on our New Jersey reader. In addition, several states have brought civil suits for alleged deceptive practices.

—June 1995

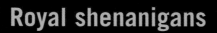

Winning your way to the poorhouse

Last fall, a Virginia reader received, unsolicited, a small box labeled "cash prize" and sent by U.S. Commemorative Fine Art Gallery, in Canton, Ohio. (That outfit is one of the many divisions of Suarez Corporation.) Inside were 30 old pennies with Lincoln on one side, wheat on the other. The company said it wouldn't tell our reader the value of the coins (except to say they were worth "at least 10 times their minted value") or release 20 extra pennies it was holding for him unless he paid $12 for a 50-coin "Protective Display." An invoice stamped "Final Notice" was included. The best part: The original 30 pennies came with $1.79 postage due.

—June 1996

Royal shenanigans

"**I**s there noble blood in your family?" asked a postcard with a return address in Queensland, Australia. The card went on to tell an Oregon reader that he was entitled to a Royal Award personally approved by his Royal Highness the Prince Regent of the Principality of Hutt River Province. The card identified his highness as Prince Kevin (Prince *Kevin*?) and stated the reasons for the honor as "service to your community, honest business dealings, or simply because of a distant blood relation." The note didn't state the nature of the Royal Award, but it's issued as a certificate whose value is "incalculable." Is it worth the $10 statutory investiture fee honorees must send to Australia (along with an affirmation that they won't "misuse or abuse the power and influence of the award")? Our reader thought not.

Maps revealed no Principality of Hutt River Province, described as a free state in the South Seas, so we called the Australian Consulate. The consul for public affairs told us the province is actually a piece of land in Western Australia owned by a former wheat farmer who quarreled with the government, "seceded," and began to sell Hutt River stamps, coins, ambassadorships, and, apparently, Royal Awards. The wheat farmer crowned himself Prince Leonard, said the consul, who added, "I haven't heard of Prince Kev."

—June 1994

Something fishy

"**D**ear Owner," said the letter from Florida-based Ewing Fairchild International Corporation, "It is our sincere pleasure to inform you that you have been chosen to receive a new ELECTRA SPORT FISHING BOAT AND OUTBOARD MOTOR as part of our latest marketing program." Ewing Fairchild asked Owners to arrange for shipment of the "fishing and recreational craft" and to pay shipping, handling, and promotional fees not to exceed $99.50. No specifications or photograph accompanied the letter.

Owners who envisioned catching marlin off Acapulco were no doubt saddened when they received the nine-foot inflatable raft shown, with an eggbeater sort of electric propeller (batteries not included).

Responding to complaints from Idaho "winners," the Idaho Attorney General's Office looked into the solicitation and found that in paying $99.50, Owners were actually buying the boat. The office ordered two boats and conducted "a Jack LaLanne test," said Brett DeLange, a deputy attorney general: "We took one of the boats to a swimming pool and tied it to an investigator. He swam one way while the motor was pushing the boat the other way." The investigator won the tug of war, pulling the boat to his side of the pool even though the engine was motoring full speed ahead.

An Idaho state court required Ewing Fairchild to stop its solicitation, reimburse any Idaho consumers who were taken in, and pay the state of Idaho penalties and fees of $17,550. The judgment applies only to Idaho; DeLange says the company may still be shipping rafts to people in other states.

—March 1994

Everyone's a winner

Funny things can happen when you let a computer address your mail. American Family Publishers recently informed a Mrs. Laughingstock of Downers Grove, Illinois, that she was about to hit the sweepstakes jackpot. "Mrs. Laughingstock," says the letter, "you've got ten million dollars coming to you. . . ."

The man who received the notice wondered how the publisher's computer decided that LaughingStock, his card and gift shop, was a Mrs. He'd better stop wondering long enough to respond: According to the Laughingstock Finalist Document, "Another finalist is waiting to walk off with Mrs. Laughingstock's ten million dollars!"

Perhaps that other lucky finalist is Dist A. Fraud. He (she?), too, is in the running for $10 million from American Family Publishers. Wichita's district attorney fraud unit could probably use the extra cash.

—April 1993

Buy or pay

"**C**ongratulations," begins the letter an Illinois reader recently received from CVP Sweepstakes Department. "YOU DEFINITELY ARE A FIRST ROUND CASH WINNER." And despite the dozens of products peddled in the mailing, from thermal socks to grandfather clocks, "There is no financial obligation—nor are you made to purchase anything. . . . [Simply] request your share of the first round cash in accordance with sweepstakes rules. That's absolutely it!"

Unless you take the next paragraph (labeled "IMPORTANT") seriously. It explains: "Since this sweepstakes is part of a campaign to promote CVP's quality line of products, please order at least two or more items." An order form—make that "Prize Claim Form"—follows.

And what of those winners who don't take the hint? A small note at the bottom of the order form refers them to "Rule #6," which hardy searchers will find on the back of the forty-second and final page in the mailing. It's a 209-word explanation of the cutting and pasting required of nonpurchasers who want to claim a prize.

Print the words DME Sweepstakes across the top of the long side of a three-by-five-inch index card or any stiff, blank, three-by-five-inch sheet of paper, says Rule #6. Carefully cut out your computer-printed name and address and affix it to the card with glue or cellophane tape (no staples or paper clips). Put the card in a plain envelope. Do not bend or fold. Do NOT use the enclosed official sweepstakes reply envelope and do NOT mail to the address on the official sweepstakes reply envelope. Finally, print the correct address correctly. After all, Rule #6 warns, "Failure to comply fully and completely with all instructions" could make even winners losers.

Kinda makes us want to fold, spindle, and mutilate.

—May 1993

Sweepstakes charade

Sometimes it seems that every mail delivery brings a postcard that says you've won a car, or money, or a cruise, or some dubious-sounding item like a "savings certificate," "diamond pendant," or " men's and ladies' sports watch."

A Pennsylvania reader recently followed up on an offer from Sweepstakes Clearinghouse of Dallas, Texas. The "official notice" promised he had "definitely been awarded" two prizes from a list that included $10,000 cash, $1,000 cash, a $100 U.S. Savings Bond, and a $200 savings certificate. There was a 900 number he could call to find out his prizes.

The two prizes turned out to be two copies of the "savings certificate," which was a $200 coupon good toward the purchase of merchandise from a small "American Home Shopper" catalog Sweepstakes Clearinghouse sent later. The catalog features houseware and electronics items marked with "reference retail" prices.

To see how realistic those prices are, we tracked down two items.

One was a Magnavox CD player marked at $389.95. Although a red blaze said it was a "New 1991 Model!" we identified it as a discontinued model from 1988. Back then, it carried a manufacturer's list price of $300. If you were able to find a comparable CD player today, perhaps at a discount store or in a catalog that deals in discounted models, it might sell for $150 or so.

Then there was a Magnavox VCR, also called a "New 1991 Model!" and priced at $449.95. Again, we found that it was really a discontinued 1988 model. A comparable machine would cost $250 or so today at discount.

Even with a $200 coupon, the prices from Sweepstakes Clearinghouse look no better than those one can find at a discount store. The contest, the awards, and the 900 number, it seems, just camouflage a mail-order discount operation.

—*January 1992*

Pushing your luck

Those sweepstakes entry forms disseminated widely and relentlessly by Publishers Clearing House, a magazine subscription agency that sells a host of publications, including *Consumer Reports,* have been assuring recipients—as the law requires—that they're eligible to win prizes even if they don't place an order. But apparently several of our readers have sorely tested PCH's patience. With the latest entry form, each received the following peevish communication: "DON'T BOTHER ENTERING IF YOU'RE NOT ORDERING! . . . although you've entered a Clearing House Sweeps 5 times, you haven't ordered a single

thing . . . we'll honor your entry this time . . . But that doesn't mean I have to keep sending you our Bulletins."

When we learned about the letter, we told PCH about our unhappiness with the way it was worded. As we went to press, PCH agreed to change the letter.

—October 1991

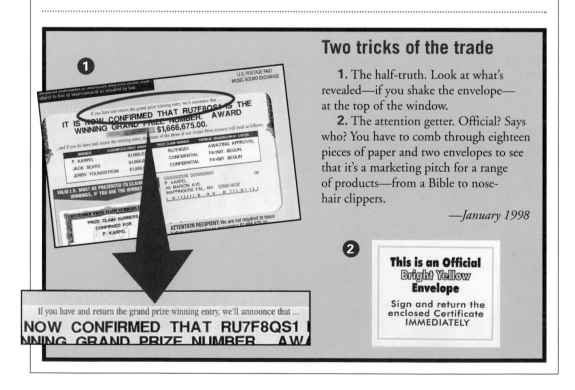

Two tricks of the trade

1. The half-truth. Look at what's revealed—if you shake the envelope—at the top of the window.

2. The attention getter. Official? Says who? You have to comb through eighteen pieces of paper and two envelopes to see that it's a marketing pitch for a range of products—from a Bible to nose-hair clippers.

—January 1998

This is an Official
Bright Yellow
Envelope

Sign and return the enclosed Certificate IMMEDIATELY

THE AUTO SHOW

"I have figured out the relation of advertising to truth. What advertising does to truth is what whipping does to cream."

C. F. "Ket" Kettering, head of
General Motors research during the 1930s

W hen the Tin Lizzy was competing with Old Dobbin, car sellers actually had to play up the differences. In 1905, a car was advertised as "simple as a pair of reins." Another early ad featured side-by-side pictures of a horse and a car. The caption under the horse: "Board, one year $180.00." Under the car: "Gasoline, one year $35.00." (Clearly, that was long ago; today, the horse might be cheaper.)

While a horse was a horse, of course, nobody was quite sure what to call a car in 1900, when they numbered eight thousand in the U.S. (and when there were less than 150 miles of paved road). Among the suggestions: autobat, autocycle, autogo, self-motor, farmobile, pneumobile, zentmobile, and ipsometer.

The Duryea brothers of Springfield, Massachusetts, who printed the first illustrated auto ad, in 1896, called their product a motor wagon. Their initial effort was a standard buggy with a one-cylinder, four-horsepower engine under its seat. (Judging by its frail looks, the owner might have been tempted to hitch a fifth, real horse up front.)

Once consumers got the concept—and once Ransom Olds, manufacturer of the Oldsmobile, produced commercial models and guaranteed they'd look alike— cars didn't need to be explained in the same way. In fact, Henry Ford concluded that print ads were a waste of money because potential buyers wanted to see what they'd be riding in. So, early on, manufacturers tried to sell cars by entering them in public races. The first was held in Illinois, on Thanksgiving Day 1895. Six cars started the fifty-four-mile course; two finished. One of the horseless carriages actually ran into a horse and hack.

Eventually, though, ads proliferated—so much so that by 1926, adman Bruce Barton could say, "Today there is no more need of advertising the details of automobiles to the American public than there is for advertising the multiplication table." As a result, he noted, "automobile advertising says nothing and has said nothing for years."

In fact, saying nothing about a car has been a selling technique off and on. One of the most famous print ads ever penned, headlined "The Penalty of Leadership," was adorned with one tiny stamplike image (of a horse and rider, of all things) and consisted of thirty lines of text that could be taken as inspiring pep talk or semiparanoid poppycock. "When a man's work becomes a standard for the whole world," it read in part, "it also becomes a target for the shafts of the envious few."

Although the copy touched on the art of Whistler, the music of Wagner, and the inventiveness of Robert Fulton, it never named the product that inspired it—the Cadillac. It ran only once, in the *Saturday Evening Post,* in 1915, but once was enough. Sales rose; and for years, an annual average of ten thousand copies of the ad were mailed on request.

"The Penalty of Leadership" prefigured the ad campaign that introduced the Infiniti to the U.S. nearly seventy-five years later. Ads showed lakeside panoramas and budding twigs (but no car), and they carried a message of harmony with nature, self-restraint, and peace of mind. *Consumer Reports* called it Zen advertising.

Other techniques used to sell cars over the years:

- *The car as personal statement.* The Paige-Jewett line of cars was said to "match milady's mode—yes, her every mood!" Jane and Michael Stern, authors of the book *Auto Ads,* went so far as to segment cars by name, as an aid to owners. People of leisure could have a Riviera, Bel Air, Malibu, Newport, or Monaco; those who liked life in the fast lane could have a Bonneville, LeMans, GTO, or Grand Prix; those with something to prove could have a Marauder, Challenger, Charger, or Javelin.

- *The car as romance object.* The Jordan Motor Car Company touted its vehicle with these words: "Somewhere west of Laramie there's a bronchobusting, steer-roping girl who knows what I'm talking about. . . . The Playboy was built for the lass whose face is brown with the sun when the day is done of revel and romp and race."

- *The car as art object.* Somehow, this worked better in olden days. A huge, beveled Chrysler looked kind of impressive when backed by the Parthenon, but a Hyundai?

- *The car as second home.* A Rolls-Royce came equipped with an Espresso machine, a dictating machine, a bed, hot and cold water for washing, an electric razor, and a phone (which was a big deal in 1963).

- *The car as medicine and income-booster.* A 1924 Ford ad said, "By stimulating good health and efficiency, owning a Ford increases your earning power."

- *The car as a manly thing.* In a 1924 Chevrolet ad, a man, arms folded, perused a line of cars. "Perhaps he is wondering why these other men of no greater physical strength or mental ability can own automobiles and *ride* towards success," the copy read, "while he plods along, year after year, not only not making progress, but actually falling behind." A Chevy could help, the ad continued, because it was "a personality multiplier, a time doubler."

- *The car as a main event.* To Willys-Overland, Inc., buying a car was one of life's big four moments. The others: marriage, buying a house, and having a baby.

- *The car as safety-mobile.* During a brief time-out in the horsepower race of the 1950s, Ford emphasized safety rather than performance. Its ads mentioned Life Guard design—a dished steering wheel, improved door locks, a rearview mirror that moved on impact, optional safety belts, and a padded dashboard. That campaign flopped, though safety seems to be working today for some car makers.

- *The car as acrobat.* In precursors to current SUV ads, a 1915 Hudson perched atop a sheared-off cliff, an ancient Cadillac muscled its way up steep stone steps, and a 1903 Oldsmobile drove through snow to transport a large Yule log from woods to hearth.

Occasionally car marketers have taken a break from the hyper-sell. When Ford was readying ads for its Model A, Edsel Ford suggested one change. "In one of the advertisements I see you use the word perfect," he's been quoted as saying. "I think it would be better to say correct. Nothing is perfect." In 1986, *Consumer Reports* found a Chevy dealer in Illinois that listed a "dirty dozen" used cars selling for

$290 to $890. The dealer's 1978 Ford Granada was said to run "on oil, not gas." Its 1978 Camaro was "used in target practice for the Coast Guard." Its 1972 Nova would "make a great planter." Its 1977 Malibu "won't make great anything." Except maybe lemonade. (Which brings us to the word "lemon." In the 1860s, it sometimes referred to a worthless person or thing. It then became a rude synonym for an unattractive woman and from there attached itself to a new car in poor condition.)

More typical than such refreshing honesty is what *Consumer Reports* saw when surveying dealer ads from newspapers in twenty-one states in 1991. Of 416 ads, only about one-third answered a simple question: What is the car, and what is the price? We found a Cadillac dealer that promised in two-inch type "40% off" 1991 Sedan De Villes and Sevilles. Nowhere did the word "used" appear. But small print noted that the 40-percent-off Seville had been driven 15,825 miles. A deal for Yugos for "only $42.40" involved taking out a home-equity loan for up to fifteen years. The payment covered only interest on the loan.

Another trick is to brag about the obvious. Chevrolet claimed that 109 advantages stopped the Chevelle from becoming old before its time. They included an outside mirror, padded sun visors, and safety and pollution measures required by law. A Mazda ad attributed the "solid road car feeling" of the 323 model to its "monocoque platform." Translation: unit-body construction, which even a 1941 Nash 600 had, and virtually every car has today.

And how about auto sellers' difficulty with the "U" word? "Preowned" was bad enough, but "executive driven"? "*Previously* driven"?

Questionable sales techniques seem to have left car dealers with a reputation that wouldn't pass an emissions test ever since they first strung those little plastic flags across a lot. In *The Grapes of Wrath,* John Steinbeck described a used-car lot whose dealers pour sawdust in the innards of one car to keep it from rattling, put a defective battery in another, and use a third as a bait-and-switch prop. "People are nice, mostly," one salesman says. "They hate to put you out. Make 'em put you out, an' then sock it to 'em. . . ."

By 1941 General Motors felt the need to sell not only its cars but its dealers. "They bring to [their] job a steadily increasing skill in management, a standard of business judgment that entitles them to recognition as one of the finest groups of merchants in America," said an ad. "They are just that, with mighty few exceptions. And they are something more. They are valuable assets to any community— good men to know as neighbors and friends."

Today, the reputation is still not what GM had hoped for. In Gallup's recent honesty and ethics poll, car salespeople were dead last on a list of dozens of jobs, as they have been since the survey began in 1977. (Rankings are based on the percent of respondents rating the occupation high or very high on honesty and ethics; car salespeople scored 7 percent.) When the National Association of

Consumer Agency Administrators and the Consumer Federation of America surveyed the top areas of consumer complaints for 2000, auto sales came in second; auto repairs fourth.

Based on recent experiences of the "Selling It" editor, today's dealers are trying a variety of approaches with buyers. At one dealer, she encountered the old-style hard sell. Phoning with one question—what sales tax applied in the dealer's state?—she was given the third degree about her choice in cars and was asked personal information until she had to ask, "Do you know the answer or not?" At dealer number two, she was left alone—to such an extent that she thought she'd wandered into a car-rental agency. Trying to determine the nature of the business, she ambled past chain-link fences and peered into cars unhindered for twenty minutes. She saw a human face only when she opened a door in the nearest building and asked if the cars were for sale. (They were.) At dealer number three, she experienced something close to Freudian analysis. She was greeted with Cheshire-cat smiles, was offered coffee, was told the sales staff's philosophy, was shown flip charts, was asked to explore her reasons for choosing the car she'd decided on long before (had she considered the merits of a competitor's vehicle?); and, after a half hour, was asked to grade her experience at the dealer so far. She never got outside the showroom. Before she could be asked about her dreams, she fled to dealer number four, at which an enthusiastic young man let her look awhile, answered questions, then let her leave without warning her she'd lost a deal. She bought there.

Whether you shop at a store or on-line, here's how to avoid driving home in a citrus fruit:

- Do your homework. Good places to start include www.autosite.com, www.ConsumerReports.org, www.edmunds.com, www.kbbcom., and the carmakers' web sites.
- Try not to fall in love with a particular car; you're apt to overpay.
- Once you've decided on a model, shop around. Don't be coaxed into naming a price or monthly payment you can't afford. Don't put down a deposit, and resist pressure to buy immediately. Keep negotiations for a new car and any trade-in separate.
- Know what the dealer paid. The Consumer Reports Wholesale Price is part of a tool kit of car information available for $12 by calling 800-269-1139.
- Figure out a fair price. Typically, you can buy models in ample supply for 4 to 8 percent over the wholesale price, but you may have to pay far more for high-demand models.
- Leasing usually makes sense only if you don't exceed the annual mileage allowance, don't terminate the lease early, keep the car in good shape, and like to trade in every two or three years. > > >

Officiously official

These examples of faux fanciness, courtesy of Lute Riley Honda in Texas, drew a laugh from a reader at the, um, Main Office for the *Receipt* of Actual Documentation. They were simply part of a promotion.

—April 1999

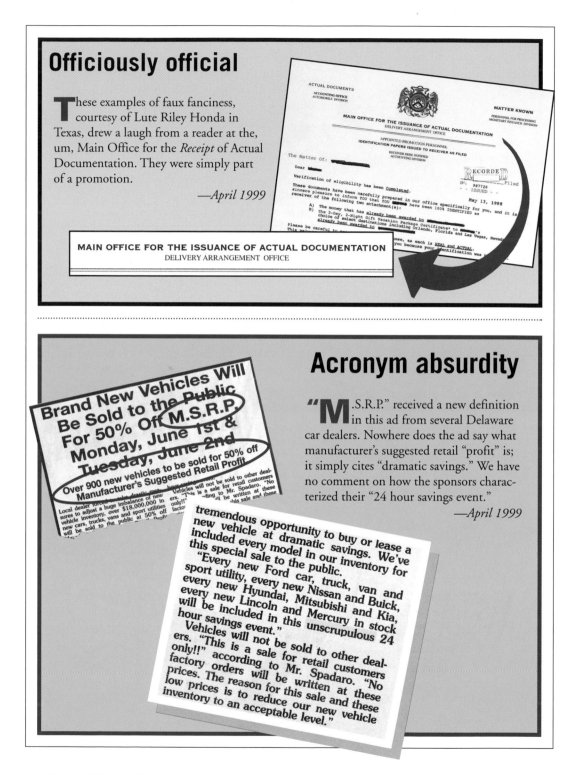

Acronym absurdity

"M.S.R.P." received a new definition in this ad from several Delaware car dealers. Nowhere does the ad say what manufacturer's suggested retail "profit" is; it simply cites "dramatic savings." We have no comment on how the sponsors characterized their "24 hour savings event."

—April 1999

A recall? Nope

The Final Reminder at right came to an Illinois reader from the Motor Vehicle Protection Corporation. And why was it "important that you call our office for information regarding your automobile"? We called and asked. "That would be in reference to extending the warranty," we were told. And the Corporation? It's a marketing agency for an insurance company.

—*June 1997*

Calling cards

Suspecting bad news about their new cars, readers in Maryland, Illinois, Ohio, Texas, and Washington fetched their owner's manual and called Toyota after receiving a card like this in the mail. Flawed transmission? Defective brakes? No, the toll-free number reached a dealership in New Jersey that was simply peddling extended-service contracts. Toyota Motor Sales, U.S.A., Inc., denies any part in the sales campaign but says the dealership is selling genuine Toyota contracts—and mailing some five thousand postcards a day. One reader, who bought a service contract from the long-distance dealer, tells us he later found the same contract for $300 less at a local Toyota shop.

—*April 1993*

Now that we've got your attention

A car recall? Nope. The ad inside recalled a reader's "attendance."

—*April 1999*

Calling all car ads

And now, a few items submitted by readers during the past year.

1. What's this "official," "registered" document from "Acquisition Headquarters"? Why, it's "an invitation to an exciting vehicle buying experience" for "the biggest Pre-Owned Acquisition Event ever held in this area." In other words, it's a form letter asking a reader to buy a used car.

2. If you did "dare to compare" prices charged by Joyce Toyota, in Illinois, with those of four other service stations, as this brochure from Joyce suggests, you might not take your car there. For the repairs Joyce lists, its prices are never cheapest. And for a minor tune-up, its listed price is highest—$22 more than that of the least expensive alternative.

—April 1998

❶

ACQUISITION HEADQUARTERS
394 Wards Corner Road, Suite 150
Loveland, Ohio 45140

REGISTERED DOCUMENTS ENCLOSED FOR ADDRESSEE ONLY. NO OTHER INDIVIDUAL SHOULD OPEN OR TAKE POSSESSION OF THE CONTENTS WHICH ARE PRIVATE AND INTENDED FOR THE PERSON INTENDED HEREIN. $2000.00 OR 5 YEARS IMPRISONMENT OR BOTH FOR ANY PERSON WHO TAMPERS OR OBSTRUCTS DELIVERY. U.S. CODE TITLE 10, SEC 1702.

OFFICIAL DOCUMENT ENCLOSED

❷

DARE TO COMPARE
And you thought Toyota dealerships were more expensive!

'02 CAMRY 4 CYL.	OIL & FILTER CHANGE	COOLING SYSTEM	MINOR TUNE-UP	BRAKE SERVICE
Speedy Lube	$19.99	$29.99	$44.99	$99.99
Firestone	$16.99	$49.99	$49.99	$89.99
Goodyear	$20.95	$49.95	$39.95	$109.00
Penske K-Mart	$21.99	$39.99	$49.99	$99.00
Joyce Toyota	$18.95	$49.95	$61.95	$104.95

FACTORY TRAINED TECHNICIANS & GENUINE TOYOTA PARTS DO MAKE A DIFFERENCE!

TOYOTA PARTS & SERVICE   ⊗ TOYOTA

It's Great. It's Anerican. It's Over Soon.

0.9% APR

EVENT

Selected models for qualified buyers through 7/2/98

It's huge. It's a typo. The sign painter's job may be over soon.

A staffer spied this billboard, for a Ford sale, in Bergenfield, New Jersey.

—April 1999

Auto roundup: Honk if you've seen ads like these

1. Do we get a steering wheel, too?

2. $0 down, but $930 due at lease signing? Here's how that sum is explained: "929.85 initial fee due at lease signing = $0 down pymt., 1st mo. pymt., $250 sec. dep. & $450 acq. fee plus taxes, title, license & registration."

3. Wow. Maybe if you buy two cars, a reader suggests, they'll throw in a doughnut.

4. This wording led a Virginia reader to speculate: Would her cost be prorated if she used only a truck's right front tire?

5. A Pennsylvania reader wondered how an "everyday low price" could have an expiration date.

6. The Virginia reader who submitted this coupon wasn't sure whether he was bringing his car to a service station or a doctor. (Staffers at our auto-test facility say such an ailment is possible only in diesel engines, not in the gasoline engines found in most cars.)

7. Did this letter from the Honda Notification Center bring a recall notice? No, only a "special Honda recall program" in which owners of late-model Hondas were asked to trade them for a new car.

—April 1997

Auto ad awards

1. The smaller print on this ominous notice, from a Philadelphia dealer, says, "We're recalling all Nissan & Mitsubishi owners who have not used our service departments for over a year."

2. The envelope with a scary message from Cross Country, a North Carolina dealer, contained a letter that "qualifies you to terminate the loan on your present vehicle." It held a $500 voucher that could be used to refinance a new car or buy a used one.

3. A Wisconsin reader could spend a lot taking his car in for free oil changes.

4. A Texas reader wondered about this ad from Fred Haas Toyota. Don't all cars have every standard feature?

5. "Obviously," said a reader from Oregon, "this car dealership's idea of a HUGE INVENTORY is not the same as mine!"

6. This BMW's price may look like a typo, but it's not—it's just wrong. A notice under the ad says, "Car shown with options package. Actual cost $22,300."

7. Official-looking papers from "Adams, Dunhill, Trump & Associates," complete with Confidential Security Seal and images of robed statuary, promised a Georgia reader a Buick Regal or cash, plus a "multi-merchandise shipment" being held in a warehouse. The material played up the car prize, even asking the reader to check desired options and color. Fine print brought him back down to earth. The odds of winning the car are unknown, the papers said; the guaranteed second prize of cash would not be less than—hold on—68 cents. And the mysterious warehoused shipment? "Prompt motor delivery" would cost our reader $22.87.

—April 1996

1 METRO NISSAN • MITSUBISHI RECALL

2 AUTO LOAN TERMINATION NOTIFICATION ENCLOSED

3 FREE Oil & Filter Change
Oil filter & up to 5 quarts of oil
$9.95
Expires 5-31-95.
scaffidi
FORD - LINCOLN - MERCURY - GMC - MACK - ISUZU
BYPASS HWY. 51 AT HWY. 66 EAST
STEVENS POINT • PHONE 344-4100

4 NEW '95 TERCEL ABSOLUTELY EVERY STANDARD FEATURE!!! 51 AVAILABLE! $8495 Stk#1390 - 1 Only

5 YEAR-END CLEARANCE! HUGE INVENTORY! 1995 JETTA
Automatic, power steering, dual air bags, alarm system, power door locks, 100,000 miles or 10-yr warranty.
1 AT THIS PRICE
$11,988
OFFER GOOD THRU MON. 10/9/95

6 ITS BODY LOOKS LIKE A SPORTS CAR. ITS PRICE LOOKS LIKE A TYPOGRAPHICAL ERROR.
$19,900 1995 BMW 318i

7 THIS IS AN OFFICIALLY REGISTERED NOTIFICATION
AFFIDAVITS ENCLOSED
CASH OR BUICK ENTITLEMENT DOCUMENTS
Official Cash Transfer And 1995 Buick Title Preference Forms Enclosed

WHAT MAKES THE FZ4 WAY COOL?
Ready? Engage. Style. Most outrageous.. Affordability. See the man. 45/50/55 series. Lower than low. All-season. Whatever. V-rated. Wired. For sports sedans and coupes. Whoa. Catch up. Plus sizing. Definitely works. Makes stellar affordable wheel/tire packages. High-impact messages. Low aspect ratio. Hello?! We're talking most excellent match here. Hey, where's it written that only Z-rated rules? They're your wheels. FZ4 is the deal. Stop dreaming.
Reality can be good.

Keen, neat-o, and far out, man

A lot of companies are looking for ways to appeal to younger buyers, but a brochure recently published by Toyo Tires seems to try a little too hard. Our auto editor and resident tire expert couldn't decipher the paragraph above. But then, he's over thirty.

—October 1996

Car wars

This ad, published in *New York Motorist* last year, led a reader to wonder how many cylinders "most cars" have, if tune-ups for fours, sixes, and eights all cost more than $34.95.

—April 1995

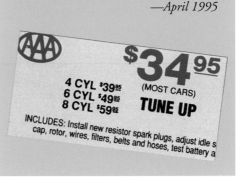

Where's the rest of me?

If you want to keep your car, Club it," says a TV ad for the Club, the antitheft device that fits over a car's steering wheel. That argument must have convinced the person who owned the car that used to be attached to the steering wheel shown here. As we've pointed out in the past, a bar lock may deter a thief, but anyone determined to steal a clubbed car can slice through the steering wheel. (Evidently this thief simply unbolted the steering wheel and found some nefarious way to maneuver the car from the curb.) This Club and wheel wound up under a tree in Brooklyn, New York. The thief got to keep the car.

—September 1994

Dirt cheap?

Tiny print is still alive and kicking in its favorite domain, auto ads. Consider Suzuki's ad for its four-wheel-drive Sidekick. Mountain rangers had trouble chasing night-driving off-roaders whose four-by-fours were harming the environment, the ad says, until the rangers began driving Sidekick four-wheel drives. And there one is, sitting atop some off-road dirt. The price? Some might assume it's $11,899, which appears in bold print next to the description of the vehicle. No, explains the minuscule message below, that's the suggested retail price for a two-wheel-drive model. According to a Suzuki dealer with whom we spoke, the four-wheel drive costs about $1,200 more.

—*September 1993*

A low ball (actually, it's in the dirt)

Our favorite auto ad of the month comes from the Ft. Lauderdale, Florida, *Sun-Sentinel,* where a Chevrolet dealership called Gary Fronrath advertises.

The ad shows six new cars with very attractive prices: a Chevrolet Astro Van for $11,468 and a Chevrolet Camaro for $9,729, for instance. The big print suggests you could buy that Camaro for $9,729 or 47 payments of $207. But notice that pesky asterisk. It directs you to a block of mouse print way down at the bottom of the page.

Teeny type explains the catch: There's a 48th payment. It's larger than the first 47. A lot larger. In the case of the Camaro, the last payment is $4,254. That lifts the price from $9,729 to $13,983.

And, oh yes, there's an unexplained "dealer services" fee. That turns out to be $399—extra money slapped onto each purchase.

—*September 1992*

Thanks (chug, sputter) but no thanks (clunk, sproing)

Last summer, after Galina and Iosif Nizhnikov's Volkswagen expired, the couple went to Sterling Ford, in Sterling, Virginia, to buy a new car. The Nizhnikovs hadn't read Sterling's ad, which said the dealer was "giving away a car a day," but when they arrived, they signed up for the giveaway—and won. Or so they thought.

The Nizhnikovs were given a choice among three cars. Three old, broken-down cars. The first was a 1985 Ford Escort with a dead battery. Sterling jump-started the battery and the car coughed into action, enabling the Nizhnikovs to ascertain that it lacked a muffler. "It made a noise like a sander," Mr. Nizhnikov told us. Sterling conceded the car needed hundreds of dollars' worth of work. Car number two was soggy, smelly—and drafty. "I looked under the seat," Mr. Nizhnikov recounted, "and you could see the ground. You didn't need an engine in this car. I could just put my feet on the ground and push it." Car number three was equally infirm.

When we called Sterling Ford, its general manager got technical. "The ad didn't say they were new cars," he pointed out. "But in the future we'll say if they're pre-owned." And what of the Nizhnikovs? They turned down all three cars, said Mr. Nizhnikov, and went to another dealer: "We bought a Mazda Protegé, which we read about in *Consumer Reports*, and we like it very much."

—*December 1992*

Sizing it up

"The only possible meaning that this slogan conveys is that 'no other van of this size is larger than this van!'" concluded the Texan who spotted this ad in his local paper.

—*April 1993*

Dodge dealers in the New York City area recently aired a series of TV commercials boasting that more than 70 percent of the owners of Toyota Corollas, Honda Civics, Ford Escorts, and Chevrolet Cavaliers actually preferred the new Dodge Shadow, according to "100 [people] surveyed." Since our own surveys of *Consumer Reports* subscribers have shown that owners of Civics and Corollas are more satisfied with their cars than are owners of Dodge Shadows, the commercial piqued

our interest. The reasons for the difference between our survey results and those reports in the Dodge commercial became clear after Chrysler Corporation described the survey's methodology to us.

A survey firm retained by Chrysler chose owners of 1988 to 1991 Civics, Corollas, Cavaliers, and Escorts to participate in an experiment. The willing respondents—about 25 for each competitor—were given an opportunity to inspect a '92 Dodge and a '92 version of the car they already owned. They were also allowed to take the Dodge—but not the other car—out for a spin. After the look-see, the 100 people were asked if they thought the Dodge was better or worse than their current car. Seventy-three

percent reportedly said the Dodge was better. Does that mean that most Civic and Corolla owners would prefer a new Dodge Shadow to a new Civic and Corolla, as the commercial implied? Probably not. Here's why.

First, of course, since the respondents were allowed to test-drive only the Dodge, not a new version of the model they owned, they were actually comparing a new car with a used one. For balance, we would like to have seen what owners of an older Dodge Shadow thought of their car after driving a new Corolla, Civic, Escort, and Cavalier.

Second, combining the opinions of owners of four different cars hides any distinctions among them. Honda Civic and Toyota Corolla owners, for example, might have preferred their own car to the Dodge Shadow, while Ford Escort and Chevrolet Cavalier owners might have strongly opted for the Dodge. One can't know from the reported result.

Finally, it's hard to believe that the respondents couldn't have guessed what the test was all about (and perhaps have wanted to please its sponsor), since they'd been promised $60 apiece to do a test that involved driving just one manufacturer's car.

—August 1992

Ladies and gentlemen, start your calculators

From our "What's the catch?" files comes a new advertising gimmick, courtesy of a couple of car dealers in the Midwest: If you buy a new car and trade in your old, they'll credit you with "100% OF ORIGINAL VALUE!!" of your trade-in. The catch, in the two ads we saw, came in bashful type that said "less 16¢ per mile and reconditioning."

Consider a 1986 Honda Accord DX. New, it cost about $11,500. If it's been driven 12,000 miles a year (72,000 miles in all), the 16-cent charge would be $11,520. Meaning the car is worth a negative $20. But according to the NADA Official Used Car Guide,

that car should trade in for about $4,300. The offer would be worth more with cars that cost more to begin with, but then other restrictions apply, such as a cap of $8,000 on any trade-in under the offer. We asked the dealers for typical "reconditioning" fees, to see how much wiggle room such fees provide them. One refused to speculate, saying, "It depends what the car needs." Another guessed that cleaning and fixing up a car for resale would reduce his trade-in offer by "as little as $200 or as much as $1,000 or more." Enough room for quite a bit of wiggling, we'd say.

—*June 1992*

Nothing special

"**W**elcome Acura owners," said the flyer from Herb Chambers, aiming to lure new customers to his Honda dealership in Burlington, Massachusetts. Among the "service specials" the flyer offered was a timing-belt replacement for $189.95. But wait. There was a footnote: "Cars with A/C, Twin Cam or PWR Steering Extra." A hundred dollars extra, it turned out. So how many Acuras aren't equipped with air-conditioning, a twin-cam engine, or power steering? According to an Acura company spokesman, none. We asked

Herb Chambers' service department, "Who gets the $189.95 price?" After a little hemming and hawing, an employee answered, "Uh, certain Honda Civics."

—*September 1991*

We buy votes

Capitol Toyota of San Jose, California, is trying to gain a reputation for customer service the old-fashioned way: by stacking the deck. The dealer recently sent a letter to its customers, explaining that they would soon receive a customer-satisfaction survey from Toyota. In return for giving Capitol Toyota a "very satisfied" in all categories, the dealer's service director promised a "Free Auto Detail." (Capitol Toyota told us a "detail" is a good cleaning, inside and out.) He even provided a sample ballot marked the "correct" way. Perhaps thinking that there might some balky respondents, he wrote, "If you feel you honestly cannot give us all 'very satisfieds,' please call either myself or your service advisor directly to let us know what we can do to earn this score."

—April 1991

The decline of standards

An ad for Continental Honda, in suburban Chicago, ballyhoos its "Gold Standard Owners Plan," a dealer pack consisting of an extended warranty, oil changes, rustproofing, and other benefits, all "yours at no additional charge."

That's followed by a shopping list of Honda Preludes and Accords. But the "Gold Standard," the tiny type at the bottom of the page reveals, is not available on those "sale-priced" cars.

—April 1991

New model from Ford

Ricart Ford in Columbus, Ohio, must have lots of pull at the Ford Motor Company. The dealer appears to have exclusive sales rights to a new, as-yet-unheralded Ford model called the Taurus II. If you think that the $9,999 "Taurus" in the ad looks suspiciously like the cheaper and smaller Ford Escort, you're right. Ricart's ad explains all in the smaller print: "Ford wants to name this new car Escort, but one look and you'll agree Taurus II is a lot closer." In a similar spirit, the small print explains the fate of the headlined 100,000-mile warranty: "P.S. The 100,000 warranty offer actually ends at noon tomorrow."

—November 1990

Myth math

This "½ price sale," advertised by Highland Park Pontiac-Honda-GMC in Highland Park, Illinois, turns out to be a double-price sale, as the second line ("the price you see is half the price you pay") states. A call to the dealer made it clear the subhead was no garble: He was selling the Mustang for double the $4,995, or $9,990; the Ford Ranger for double the $3,995, or $7,990; and so on.

—April 1990

★ ★ ★ ★ ★ ★ ★ ★ ★ ★ ★ ★ ★ ★ ★ ★ ★ ★ ★ ★

CHAPTER 10

SIZE MATTERS

"How has it happened that a population which is aware of the odds against drawing an inside straight, which is accustomed to the handicaps in sports, which is familiar with Dow Jones averages, seems unable to remember how many pints there are to a gallon or how many ounces to a pound?"

Consumer Reports, September 1960

The answer to that question, said Joseph J. Seldin, author of *The Golden Fleece,* is that when you have the money, you let the advertiser do the menial counting. That's the easy way out, but it also opens the door to deception. As Dexter Masters, a former editor of *Consumer Reports,* noted in 1965, "Almost the entire packaging industry, with its near total confusion of sizes and shapes and weights, is a labor of love on the seller's part for the mindless buyer." Manufacturers have a little toolbox of tricks they can use to create such confusion.

They can, for instance, become a contender for what "Selling It" calls the Black Hole Award. You open a box, jar, or can, peer inside, and discover a little of the product plus a lot of air or water. We've seen diet bars that took their name to heart, rattling around in large wrappers inside an even larger box; mint wafers hemmed in by extra cardboard that was conveniently hidden by a colored wrapper; pills wedged into the bottom of their bottle by a cloud of cotton; six inches of cookies in a box nine and a half inches tall. When we opened cans of sliced peaches, we found about half the weight was usually liquid. (Sometimes the manufacturer actually helps out by printing the equivalent of "kick me" on its package: A note on the wrapping around a stick of Mitchum deodorant announced, "This handy 1 oz. container holds ½ oz."

Federal regulations allow extra space—officially, "slack fill"—for one of several reasons: Because machinery can't fill a box or bottle all the way, because some products settle, or because, as with soda, topping off could be unsafe. Sometimes boxes are big to allow better labeling or to prevent pilfering. And sometimes extra packaging helps keep fragile foods like potato chips from breaking. When it comes to canned foods, the FDA requires only a few, such as olives in brine, to reveal their weight after draining. For other types, there's wiggle room (cans of solid tuna labeled six ounces, for instance, can contain about four and a half ounces of tuna after oil or water has been squeezed out).

On the other hand, regulations prohibit empty space that serves no purpose. As an administrative law judge pointed out in a 1974 decision, the "ordinary person with a common degree of familiarity with industrial civilization would expect a reasonable relationship between the size of package and the size of quantity of the contents. He would have no reason to anticipate slack filling."

A cousin to the Black Hole Award is the Golden Cocoon, bestowed on products that disguise their size in layers of outerwear. There's been some good news on this front, with CD long boxes dieting down to jewel boxes and hamburger chains using thin paper wrapping instead of styrofoam. But catalog companies may still overpack, whether by, say, filling a box the size of a microwave oven with plastic peanuts to ship a wristwatch or by sending items ordered at the same time in separate boxes.

The size disguise carries over into the words companies use on products. Large used to mean, well, big; but now it may be small. Let's look at olives. Does their size stop at large? No. Extra large? Nope. There are two bigger sizes: colossal and super colossal. When last heard from, olives were clearly aiming for a designation of intergalactic. At least olive sizes are defined by the government; most food packages can designate their own size. A *Consumer Reports* reader who often bought a 48-ounce bag of peanut M&Ms with no size designation went back to the store for a replacement. He found a new bag that weighed 44 ounces, was smaller in dimension than the previous version—and was marked Extra Extra Large. A Canadian corn flakes fan apparently caught Kellogg's in midmetamorphosis. The two cereal boxes he bought were identical in size, yet one was labeled Family and the other Regular.

Companies may also redefine perfectly good weights and measures. A King-Seeley thermos bottle was supposed to keep "a quart of liquid hot or cold all day." A quart is 32 fluid ounces, but the label defined a King-Seeley quart as .90 liters, or 30.3 fluid ounces. Likewise, a "gallon" of Royal Islander paint was labeled as 3 quarts, 1 pint, and 14 ounces. Industry-wide, 2-by-4-inch lumber became 1⅞ by 3⅞, then was further shaved, to 1¾ by 3⅞. The one-pound coffee can contained 13 ounces by the early 1990s; today some coffee cans weigh 11.5 ounces.

When a product gets smaller but not cheaper, it's said to have downsized. That's a move you're likely to notice only if you're a regular buyer. *Consumer Reports* scored downsizing as "one of the most rapidly expanding shady practices" in 1960. Forty years later, consumer-protection officials have noted downsizing in items as diverse as cocoa and canned fish, spaghetti sauce and potato chips, soup mixes, toilet paper, and pet food. Readers have complained of disappearing acts in Sure deodorant, Cut-Rite waxed paper, Charmin toilet paper, and Breyer's ice cream. And they're ceaselessly suspicious of detergents whose scoops seem to get bigger with each new package.

Sometimes shape-shifting involves enough parameters that it's hard to tell just what is going on. A reader bought two boxes of Oatmeal Crisp. One was marked 21.5 ounces; the other had the same dimensions, said "20% more free," and was labeled, in nearly unreadable letters, 19.25 ounces.

When queried about such moves, manufacturers often point out that it's the retailer who sets the product's price; or that trimming an ounce here and there helps stave off price hikes; or that the detergent's formula has changed; or that the new toilet paper is thicker so you need fewer sheets; or that the smaller soap is easier to hold; or that consumers actually prefer the downsized size. (When Gerber reduced the size of its "junior dinners," it said tests showed parents preferred the smaller jars three to one.)

Companies that downsize try their best to make the new, lighter version look as big as the old—a trick worth boasting about, in the case of one hand-lotion manufacturer. Its news release, quoted in *Modern Packaging*, noted: "A relatively tall, graceful bottle was modeled that in a 5-ounce size actually gives the appearance of being larger than the old 10-ounce size."

Other packages start out small on purpose. Companies learned long ago that buyers can have strong ideas about the most convenient sizes for certain products. In 1928, Richard Franken and Carroll Larabee, authors of *Packages That Sell,* said it was well known that people would rather pay ten cents for four ounces of baking soda than 25 cents for a full pound. A more recent example is the Classico line of pasta sauces. "The jars are smaller than those of competing sauces, to suggest preciousness," wrote Thomas Hine in *The Total Package,* "and the prices a little bit higher. The jars also encourage reuse for storage and thus reduce the guilt induced by throwing things away."

Sure, good things can come in small packages—but it would be nice if, once in a while, those packages trimmed their price along with their size. > > >

Packing to price— with a vengeance

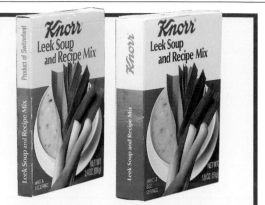

Manufacturers often try to avoid a straightforward price increase for fear that consumers may not judge the product to be worth any more than they had been paying. One way to avoid the appearance of a price increase is to reduce the size of the package while holding the price steady—the incredible shrinking Hershey bar is a familiar example. Now the makers of Knorr soup have come up with an ingenious twist.

The smaller box of Knorr Leek Soup cost a Houston reader $1.39, and held enough dry soup mix to make four 8-ounce servings. The newer and bigger box also cost $1.39. More for the money? Nope. Inside the bigger box is enough mix to make only three 8-ounce servings. The bigger box hides a 33 percent price increase.

—*August 1990*

Nothing to purr about

Heinz recently changed the shape of Pounce cat treats from triangles to hearts. But that's not all: The company also lowered the weight, from four ounces to three, while leaving the size of the container and the ingredients list identical. (Our staffer in charge of counting informs us that the new container we bought held 69½ treats; the old one, 83.) We called Heinz's consumer line and asked about the downsizing. "We appreciate that you picked up on this," a representative said—with a straight face, apparently. "We made the change to stay competitive with others in the market." She added that Heinz had also lowered the price of Pounce, to $1.19. Told that we paid $1.49 (the same price as for the old container), she noted that stores can set their own price and suggested we shop around.

—*July 1997*

Soft-drink makers package water. Match manufacturers package fire. Quick, now: Who packages air?

Why, cereal manufacturers, of course.

Take Kellogg's Nutri-Grain Wheat cereal. The old box, sold until last fall, measured 9¼ x 6⅝ x 2⅛ inches and contained 12 ounces of cereal. The new box is 1⅜ inches higher and contains 12.2 ounces of cereal. Net result: The volume of the box has grown nearly 15 percent, but the amount of cereal in the box has increased by less than 2 percent.

The slogan across the front of the box: "new larger size." Clearly, it's the box, more than the product, that's larger.

A Kellogg representative told us the box had been enlarged because "product quality was being sacrificed" with the old box. How? Apparently, the flakes were being crushed. The old box bears a copyright date of 1983; the new box, 1989. Did Kellogg foist crushed flakes on its customers for half a dozen years?

—*April 1990*

Less of what counts

At first, a North Carolina reader and fan of Chiquita's Pineapple Guava Mango Juice didn't see the difference between the old container (left) and the new (right). On closer inspection, he saw the "New Improved" banner. And he noticed something else: While the old product was 100 percent juice, the new product is 20 percent juice.

Why the change? A representative at Citrus World, the distributor, explained that the price of the "bulk product"—juice—had risen so much that the company could either raise the price much higher or lower the quantity of juice. It chose option number two. And what's improved? "The company had taste tests run by an outside group," the representative said. "They seemed to think the taste was very good." Since our reader paid the same price for both cartons despite the drastic drop in juice content, he thinks the major improvement was to Chiquita's bottom line.

—August 1997

Add noodles, subtract water

"On my last trip to the supermarket," a Pennsylvania reader wrote last May, "I was delighted to find that Lipton now offered a chicken soup mix with extra noodles. Their standard chicken soup cost 99 cents, while the extra noodle version cost $1.19. Since my 3-year-old is fond of the noodles, I immediately purchased the extra noodle version." Indeed, the extra noodle soup weighs 0.4 ounce more than the regular version—4.9 ounces vs. 4.5. (Both list noodles as the first ingredient.) But the difference that led our reader to "Selling It" lay in the extra noodle soup's instructions. They call for adding less water—3 cups per pouch versus 4. With less water, of course, even the regular soup would seem more noodley.

—November 1996

Pretzel logic

The Stew Leonard's store in Connecticut sells both these bags for $1.69. Which is the better buy? Before you choose the "jumbo bag" of thin twist pretzels over the "economy size" bag of mini pretzels, it pays to check the weight. The big bag weighs 14 ounces; the little one, a pound. In other words, the jumbo bag is just that—a bigger bag. The moral: As long as you don't get bent out of shape by mini pretzels, choose them.

—*July 1998*

Product shrinks, package grows

Last year, a Massachusetts reader writes, he bought St. Ives Swiss Formula Natural Soothing Aloe Deodorant in the "NEW! 3.5 oz. Value Size." This year, he bought the same product, now in a "NEW! 3.25 oz. Value Size." Leaving aside questions of value, is the smaller stick at least in a smaller container? Nope. In fact, as our reader's photos show, the new container is bigger. The reason: Its cap is taller.

—*March 1997*

A raspberry for Minute Maid

A Pennsylvania reader sent us these 12-ounce cans of frozen concentrate for raspberry lemonade. The cans cost the same, but the newer one makes less lemonade. (The older can is the one labeled New; the newer can is the one with New Easy-to-Mix Directions.) While the older can called for an additional 4⅓ cans of water, resulting in 64 ounces of lemonade, the newer one calls for only 3 cans of water, resulting in 48 ounces—25 percent less.

When we asked Coca-Cola Foods, maker of Minute Maid, what was going on, a customer-service representative said that the product's formula was changed because the cost of ingredients had gone up. "Otherwise, we would have had to charge more," she noted.

By changing the concentration, Minute Maid is still charging more—it just takes longer for consumers to figure that out.

—October 1994

Peter, Peter, pita eater

Reader Peter pondered this packaged pair of Mr. Pita perforated pocket-bread, proffered for the same price. Which pita-pocket package did Peter pick?

Peter, who had purchased the six-pack product previously, picked the newer, twelve-pocket package, piqued by the prospect of twice the pitas for the price. Pow! Inside were the usual six round pitas semicut into semicircles. Apparently, the manufacturer had simply devised a different method of counting.

Peter was peeved.

—June 1994

Good news for suckers

As several readers pointed out, the most obvious improvement in the "new improved" version of Velamints is the reduction in weight from 0.85 ounces to 0.71 ounces—a 16 percent lightening of the mint-toter's load. For a clue to less obvious improvements, we phoned Ragold, Velamints' maker. The company says it has added more mint to the peppermint and wintergreen flavors, and more cocoa powder to the cocoa-mint. As for the weight loss? "Consumer research showed that people wanted more contoured edges and didn't want the center to melt first when sucked," said a Ragold spokesperson, "so we filled in the center and rounded off the edges." Nothing like a little chiseling around the edges.

—*February 1993*

A Fig Newton of the imagination

Below right is the new fat-free version of Nabisco's Fig Newtons. What caught our eye was the svelteness of its package. Although that package looks the same size as the fatter Fig Newtons', it weighs 12 ounces, not 16. Since both packages cost the same, that's effectively a 33 percent jump in price.

Moreover, there are only 18 cookies per package instead of 32. And even the original Fig Newtons is hardly a fatty—each cookie has only one gram of fat, which represents just 15 percent of its calories.

But wait. The premium paid for the fat-frees does give you a bonus: Because the individual cookies are a bit larger, you get 10 more calories per cookie.

—*May 1992*

Last month we sniffed at Mennen's Speed Stick, deviously downsized with less product packed in a larger container. Not being partial, we now draw your attention to Fabergé's Brut deodorant spray. The can and price have stayed the same size while the contents have dropped from five ounces to four. The new, small size proclaims "Now More Brut!" How is that possible? The company says the new size has "more fragrance." Oh. So now more means less. But smellier. Makes scents.

—*March 1992*

Hidden price increase of the month

A reader paid $1.09 for a bottle of calcium tablets (left) from an F&M drugstore, a chain with outlets in Maryland, Minnesota, and Michigan. Several weeks later, she writes, she bought the larger bottle (right) from the same store for $1.99. Both bottles contain 60 tablets.

—*November 1990*

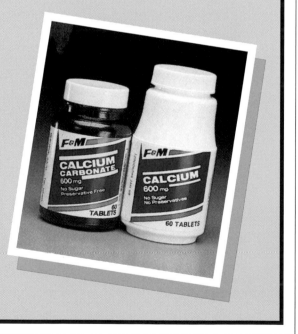

Less bountiful

In January 1988 we criticized Procter & Gamble's Bounty paper towels: P & G had reduced the size of a roll from 85 square feet to 70 in four stages while maintaining the same price. A Georgia reader sent us labels from two Bounty towels of recent vintage. They've shrunk again, from 67 to 60 square feet. (Apparently, a 70-to-67 step occurred while we weren't watching.) Despite its smaller size, and the fact that it has fewer sheets, the new roll costs the same as the old, our reader said.

But wait. Maybe the new roll is better. It features the words "More absorbent than ever." Does it absorb anything besides a few extra pennies? When we asked Procter & Gamble, a spokesperson said the new towels are 10 percent more absorbent than the old, so one can use less towel. (We have this vision of the frugal consumer carefully tearing off 10 percent less Bounty than usual while running to clean up a spill.)

Another spokesperson gave us another reason for the reduction: to maintain "consistent prices" as manufacturing costs rose. That's plausible because it's consistent with the artful dodge called "packaging to price."

Recently, P & G introduced Big Roll Bounty, with 90 square feet. Not much bigger than ordinary Bounty was three short years ago.

—August 1991

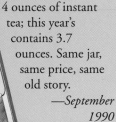

A lemon from Lipton

Readers love to point out to "Selling It" how manufacturers reduce a product's size but keep the package and price the same. This month's entry is a brand-new jar of instant tea that "makes 20 quarts," according to the label. In back, the label says you "add four rounded teaspoons to cold water" to make a quart. Last year's jar said those things, too. But last year's jar contained 4 ounces of instant tea; this year's contains 3.7 ounces. Same jar, same price, same old story.

—September 1990

New

60 SQ. FT. · 72 TWO-PLY SHEETS · 11 X 11 IN.

Old

67 SQ. FT. · 80 TWO-PLY SHEETS · 11 X 11 IN.

Let's get small

This is a full-sized photograph of the warranty registration "card"—actually a slip of paper—for a Unisonic calculator. The flip side asks that you affix a stamp.

Even if you managed to squeeze your name and address on the slip, the Post Office could refuse to deliver it. Postal regulations specify that a piece of mail be at least 3½ by 5 inches.

—*November 1991*

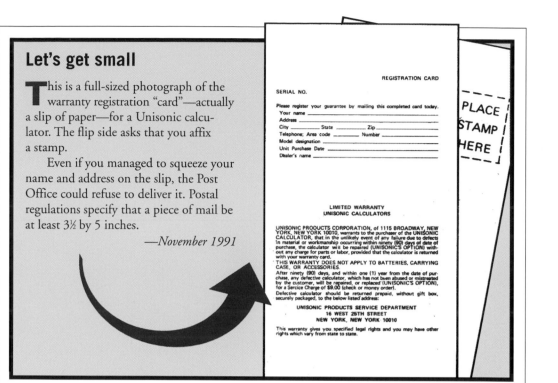

The landfill will smell nice

Our Golden Cocoon award for over-wrapping goes this month to Clinique facial soap. Getting at the soap is like battling an artichoke. You open a box, then a corrugated cardboard sleeve, then a plastic container, then a foil pack. Finally you reach a six-ounce bar. The color-coordinated wrapping doesn't come cheap. Our Clinique bar cost $9.50.

—*June 1992*

No corn-o-copia

"Looks B-I-G! Holds Very Little!" That's the boast for Cone-O-Corn, advertised in a catalog from Cincinnati-based Gold Medal Products Company. The catalog offers popcorn vendors an array of tubs, boxes, and bags. But what profiteer worth his or her salt would order those when Cone-O-Corn draws more cash per kernel from unsuspecting kids? As the ad explains, "The long tapered cone is easy for kids to hold and, of course, makes it look like it holds more than it really does—remember it is taller than bags, cups, or boxes!" Heck, it even "looks bigger than a #2053 bag, yet holds less—way less!"

—*July 1993*

"Maybe," a reader writes, "they could just simplify things and call them 'Preemie peas!'"

—*May 1994*

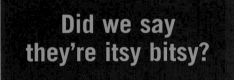

SUPER G™
VERY YOUNG SMALL EARLY PEAS

NET WT 14 OZ (396 g)

A rap on wrapping

How much wrapping does it take Philips Electronics to announce that its light bulb has won an award? Two cardboard boxes, a cardboard shell, shrink wrap, bubble wrap, and the light bulb itself. And the award this mailing announced? 1998's World Environment Center's Gold Medal.

—*August 1998*

Through thick and thin

Here are old and new versions of Betty Crocker's Chocolate Peanut Butter Bars. The new bars, the box points out, are thicker. Want to guess one reason why? . . . Time's up. The old box gave you the option of using a 13x9-inch pan for "regular" bars or a 9-inch-square pan for "extra-thick" bars. The new box tells you to use an 8- or 9-inch-square pan. The old box weighed 1 pound 6.75 ounces. The new box weighs 7 ounces less, but if you use the 8-inch-square pan, it will give you more batter per square inch than you'll get with the 13x9-inch pan. Voilà: thicker (and fewer) peanut butter bars.

—December 1996

A truly farsighted manufacturer

This Lifetime Replacement Guarantee (at least that's what we think it says) is shown actual size. It was attached to, of all things, a pair of reading glasses.

—October 1999

CHAPTER 11

'NUFF SAID

"The trade of advertising is now so near to perfection that it is not easy to propose any improvement."

Dr. Samuel Johnson, 1759

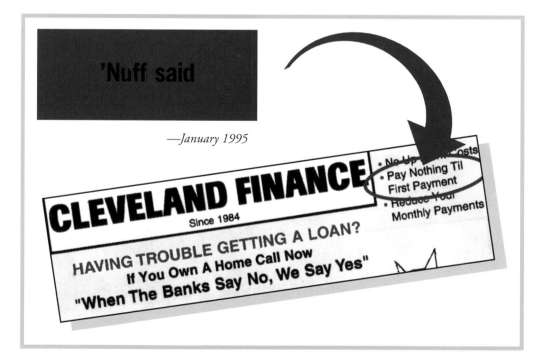

'Nuff said

—*January 1995*

CLEVELAND FINANCE
Since 1984

HAVING TROUBLE GETTING A LOAN?
If You Own A Home Call Now
"When The Banks Say No, We Say Yes"

- No Up Front Costs
- Pay Nothing Til First Payment
- Reduce Your Monthly Payments

The new boxes are here!

—February 1998

Wanted:
a chain saw
and a large truck

—October 1992

Truth in advertising?

—August 1993

92% FRESH

NOBODY SELLS FOR LESS!

$139

19" COLOR TELEVISION

ZENITH, RCA, MAGNAVOX - 19" WITH REMOTE CONTROL....$169

REMANUFACTURED WITH FULL 180 DAY WARRANTY. LIMITED QUALITY

COMPARE ANYWHERE

LIMITED QUALITY

Service

Silver Platter Center Cut
Boneless Pork Chops lb. $3.49

92% Fresh
All White Meat Ground Turkey lb. $1.99

With Bread Stuffing
Cornish $1.49

Kellogg's
APPLE CINNAMON SQUARES
Mini-Wheats
WHOLE GRAIN WHEAT SQUARES WITH APPLE CINNAMON FILLING
SMUCKER'S
SAME CEREAL! NEW BOX!
NET WT. 16.5 OZ. (1 LB 5 OZ) 468 g

PABIAN
FREE TAN!
WITH THIS COUPON (First Visit)
Tan A Round
Eastgate Shopping Center
Creighton at 9th
TAN·A·ROUND
ADVANCED TANNING SYSTEM
Suncrest Company

What a concept!

—September 1996

No word on how much a McDonald's foot-held sandwich might cost.

—March 1998

We'll take a jacket and a hundred-dollar bill, please

—March 1999

A great buy at twice the price!

—September 1997

★ ☆ ★ ☆ ★ ☆ ★ ☆ ★ ☆ ★ ☆ ★ ☆ ★ ☆ ★ ☆ ★ ☆ ★ ☆ ★ ☆ ★ ☆ ★ ☆ ★

WHO YA GONNA CALL?

Below, a small sampling from the long roster of groups that have some say over selling. Phone numbers and web sites are current as of 2001.

Federal Trade Commission

Established in 1914, the FTC has had periods of power—during which it was dubbed "the National Nanny" by critics—and slumps, particularly during the mid-1980s. By 2000, having issued its first order of corrective advertising in twenty-four years, it seemed to be flexing a little muscle again. It remains to be seen whether there will be a major change in direction under the new administration.

The FTC is prompted to investigate by complaints it has received from a company's competitors or from consumers (once complaints about a specific company reach critical mass), by reports in the media, or by the observations of its own monitors. It also stages "sweeps" and Internet surf days to net ne'er-do-wells. Often, these operations have catchy names: Project Field of Schemes (investment fraud), Operation Trip Trap (deceptive vacation offers), Operation Eraser (fraudulent credit-repair firms), and so on.

If an investigation concludes that a violation of the law exists, the FTC will issue a complaint. At that point, advertisers may comply voluntarily without admitting wrongdoing. If they resist, an administrative law judge will hold a hearing that can lead to a cease-and-desist order. Such orders become final unless they're appealed to the commission. Commission decisions, in turn, are subject to appeal through federal courts. Cease-and-desist orders prohibit companies from engaging in the alleged illegal practices. When final, these orders act as permanent injunctions. Penalties for violating consent agreements or cease-and-desist orders can include prison sentences, corrective ads, and fines for continued violations. The FTC can also seek to recover money for consumers who were deceived.

Information:

Federal Trade Commission
CRC-240
Washington, DC 20580
1-877-FTC-HELP (382-4357)
www.ftc.gov

U.S. Food and Drug Administration

The FDA can take action when a food, drug, cosmetic, or medical device sold in interstate commerce is misbranded or uses false or misleading claims in its labeling (which includes literature that accompanies the product). The agency can also act against such products if they are dangerous or, in the case of drugs, ineffective, and against products that are sold before complying with certain premarket requirements. When it finds wrongdoing, the FDA can seek voluntary correction, have the product seized, obtain an injunction, or initiate criminal prosecution.

Even the FDA has said it uses a priority system to deal with health fraud, dividing products into those that pose a direct risk (they result in injuries or adverse reactions) or indirect risk (they don't cause harm but may keep people away from proven treatment). To quote from *FDA Consumer* magazine: "Many fraudulent products may escape regulatory scrutiny."

Information:

U.S. Food and Drug Administration
5600 Fishers Lane
Rockville, MD 20857
1-888-INFO-FDA (463-6332)
www.fda.gov

U.S. Department of Agriculture

The USDA regulates the labeling of meat and poultry.

Information:

U.S. Department of Agriculture
14th and Independence Ave., SW
Washington, DC 20250
202-720-2791
www.usda.gov

U.S. Postal Service

The USPS can block money or product orders from reaching someone who has used the mail to defraud. Report fraud to your local postmaster or nearest postal inspector. For more information, visit *www.usps.com*.

Securities and Exchange Commission

The SEC deals with investor fraud. Consumers can file complaints about problem brokers or firms, for example, or Internet fraud.

Information:

SEC Complaint Center
450 Fifth St., NW
Washington, DC 20549
www.sec.gov

State Attorneys General

States have their own consumer-protection laws (sometimes referred to as "little FTC Acts") and have been especially active against sweepstakes promotions.

Information:

Contact your state attorney general's office (local telephone directory) or visit *www.FindLaw.com*, which provides links to state attorneys general after you've clicked on U.S. State Resources, then More State Resources.

Council of Better Business Bureaus

Complaints about national advertising may go to this organization's National Advertising Division (NAD), created in 1971. It takes on about 100 to 150 cases per year. Usually, the complaints consist of one company griping about another's unfair ads. If one of the companies isn't satisfied with an NAD decision, it can appeal to the National Advertising Review Board (NARB), which assembles a panel of industry execs and members of the public to render its own findings. This is basically a self-policing enterprise, but if a company fails to comply with a ruling, the case may go to the FTC.

Problem is, by the time this self-policing process has ground to a halt, the contested ad campaign has usually run its course, resulting in such outcomes as: NARB finds Acme's ad misleading and says Acme should stop running it; Acme says no way, its ad is not misleading; Acme also says it stopped running the ad last November.

Other chances for one company to rat on another come via the Lanham Act, which protects trademarks and allows competing companies to sue each other privately over false advertising, and the court system. (One company can simply sue another, which is what happened several years ago, when Pizza Hut went up against Papa John's, another chain.)

Information:

The Council of Better Business Bureaus
4200 Wilson Blvd., Suite 800
Arlington, VA 22203
703-276-0100
www.bbb.org
Or contact the nearest office (local telephone directory)

Other Resources

State department of health (local telephone directory)

State, county, and city consumer protection offices (local telephone directory). They mediate complaints, conduct investigations, prosecute offenders of consumer laws, license and regulate a variety of professionals, provide educational materials, and advocate in the consumer interest.

Consumer Action Handbook. No cost. To order, call 888-8 PUEBLO (878-3256); or visit *www.pueblo.gsa.gov.*

Consumers Union. Publisher of *Consumer Reports;* tests products and services and provides buying advice. For a list of publications, see any issue of *Consumer Reports.* For more information, contact Consumers Union, 101 Truman Ave., Yonkers, NY 10703, 914-378-2000; or visit *www.consumerReports.org.*

The National Consumers League. A nonprofit organization; works to protect and promote the economic and social interests of consumers. In 1992, it established the *National Fraud Information Center,* to which you can report fraud on the telephone or Internet. Contact NCL, 1701 K Street, NW, Suite 1201, Washington, DC 20006, 202-835-3323; or visit *www.nclnet.org.* Contact NFIC, 800-876-7060; or visit *www.fraud.org.*

The U.S. Consumer Gateway. At *www.consumer.gov.* Maintained by the FTC; provides access to consumer information from a broad range of federal information resources available on line.

Know Fraud. A public-private partnership of the U.S. Postal Inspection Service, Council of Better Business Bureaus, Department of Justice, Federal Trade Commission, National Association of Attorneys General, and other groups. For tips or questions, or to report a crime, call 877-987-3728 or visit *www.consumer.gov/knowfraud.*

The Centers for Disease Control and Prevention. Offers advice on many medical conditions. Visit *www.cdc.gov.*

www.healthfinder.gov. Developed by the U.S. Department of Health and Human Services; can lead you to online publications, clearinghouses, databases, government agencies, and nonprofit groups with reliable information on health-related topics.

Agency for Healthcare Research and Quality. A Public Health Service agency in the Department of Health and Human Services; offers medical news and advice. Call 800-358-9295 or visit *www.ahrq.gov/clinic.*